Dance Studio
SECRETS

65 Ways To Build A Thriving Studio

CLINT SALTER

© 2019 Clint Salter

Published by Clint Salter Pty Ltd
Dance Studio Owners Association
hello@dsoa.com
www.dsoa.com

Cataloguing-in-Publication entry is available from the National Library of Australia

ISBN: 978-0-9945610-2-2 (paperback)
               978-0-9945610-3-9 (ebook)

Other Titles by the Author:
Dance Studio Transformation (2016)

For Mel Rufus. Without you, there would be no Dance Studio Owners Association. You bring light and joy to not only the lives of our members but to my life daily. Thank you for everything that you do.

CONTENTS

Introduction

'If you feel like there's something out there that you're supposed to be doing, if you have a passion for it, then stop wishing and just do it.' ~ Wanda Sykes

"What do you want to be when you grow up?" I remember being asked this question often during my childhood years. My answer changed from being the blue Power Ranger to the green Power Ranger, a Japanese translator, a famous musical theater actor, the host of a cooking show... and even a Spice Girl.

I have yet to become any of these things. I have let go of my Power Ranger dream, can only say, "What is your favorite subject?" in Japanese, my singing voice went when my voice broke, I really despise cooking and I reached out to the Spice Girls to replace Posh in their tour. Shockingly, they declined.

But none of these things matter, because today I'm doing something that is my life's purpose. I'm a teacher. It's my passion! It's why I was put on this planet and, while every day isn't joyous, most of them are.

And because you're reading this book, I'm guessing that you're a teacher too. My definition of a teacher is someone who inspires, challenges, encourages, supports, and who motivates action and belief within another person.

As a dance studio owner, you do this daily for your teachers, staff, students, and parents.

What was your journey into studio ownership? Like me, you may have been a dancer, turned dance teacher, turned studio owner. While many see this as a natural progression, the reality is that making the move from being a dance teacher then going home and transitioning into a dance studio owner is way more difficult than you might think. That's why my team at the Dance Studio Owners Association and I created *Dance Studio Secrets.*

This book is a collection of dance studio ownership journeys from owners all around the globe at different stages of their business. We are pulling back the curtains to give you an up close and personal look into how other studio owners are creating thriving businesses and fulfilling lives inside and outside of the studio.

In the coming pages you will read about the tough realities of owning a dance studio, including the challenges and the times when giving up seemed like the only option, along with the road these studio owners took to get them to the light at the end of the tunnel.

You will be inspired by their big business and life wins accomplished along the way. You'll also enjoy learning about the path they took toward becoming the go-to studio in their local area.

Whether you're a new studio owner or you've been on this journey for 20 years, *Dance Studio Secrets* will help you get to that next level. You could be looking at how to bring new students into your studio or you're seeking out ways to systemize your business so you're not working 24/7. We have you covered.

In my first book, *Dance Studio Transformation*, I gave you the formula for building a studio that thrives on all levels. Today I'm sharing the stories from studio owners from every corner of the globe who have built their version of success and paved a path forward to create a dance studio that is aligned to their values, provides for their family, and creates a huge impact on their local community.

From reading this book, our aim for you is that you will fill up your notebook with ideas and follow that up by implementing an action plan on how you're going to create more success in your life and business. Get out your favorite highlighters, colored pens and a notebook... it's time to get to work!

Wishing you all the best on your journey to building a dance studio that brings you immense joy, financial freedom, and one that impacts the lives daily of your local community.

Clint

Founder & CEO
Dance Studio Owners Association
www.dsoa.com

A BONUS FOR YOU!
Go to the next level and get my bonus video training on studio growth. Post a picture of you with this book on Instagram using the hashtags #studioceo #DSOA and tag
@dancestudioownersassociation
and we'll be sure to send you this bonus training through direct message.

I have so much admiration for Hillary and her ability to juggle multiple successes at one time without letting any of the balls fall on the ground. Her stamina to keep growing and innovating in her business while raising four boys is hugely inspiring. When I started planning Dance Studio Secrets, I knew right away that I wanted to share Hillary's story.

Hillary Parnell is the CEO of the Academy for the Performing Arts and Preschool for the Arts in North Carolina, USA.

Hillary's love for logistics and creative revenue streams has enabled her to become the go-to studio in her area. With over 700 students, 50 employees, and a business that practically runs itself, she is now able to take time to create programs to help other studio owners find their own success.

Her latest projects include Dance Photo Pro, an online course to help studio owners bring dance class pictures in-house, and Dancers in Balance, a guide for studio owners to use journal activities to help their students find mental, physical and emotional well-being.

She holds a Bachelor of Science degree in Biology and Chemistry and has been featured in *Dance Studio Life* magazine, been awarded the Think Apex Award for dedicated service to her community, received numerous other community awards of excellence.

She is married and lives with her husband and four young boys in Raleigh, North Carolina. She is an avid photographer and sometimes enjoys playing tennis and teaching dance.

Check out Hillary's latest studio news at apanc.com

Chapter One

WHERE PASSION MEETS PROFIT: HILLARY PARNELL

Academy For The Performing Arts

YOU ORIGINALLY STUDIED TO BE A DENTIST – WHERE DID THE LEAP FROM DENTISTRY TO DANCE STUDIO CEO COME FROM?
My story is a little different to most studio owners I know. I didn't go to college for dance, and growing up I mostly danced recreationally.

I went to college to be a dentist. I have a biology and a chemistry degree from UNC in Chapel Hill but when I got a job out of college, I felt that it wasn't going to be my path. The market crashed in 2001 and the company I worked for went under, so I had to move back in with my parents.

I come from a very entrepreneurial family; my dad owns lots of different kinds of businesses, my sister owns a business and so I was trying to come up with a business, but I didn't quite know what it was going to be. In the back of my mind I had always wanted to own a dance studio, but I thought that it was going to be something I did in retirement, for fun.

I didn't think you could make a living as a dance studio owner. I thought it was a hobby that you did once you were married to a millionaire and just had free time and money (because of course, that's how 22-year-olds think). My dad ended up co-signing for a $50,000 line of credit and let me live at home for about three years while I got started.

From there we grew really fast, at the end of my first year I had 140 dancers and just kept growing.

WHAT WERE THE BIGGEST SURPRISES FOR YOU DURING YOUR FIRST 12 MONTHS AS A STUDIO OWNER?

To be honest I was surprised people signed up! I was so young, didn't really know what I was doing and I hired teachers right from day one because I didn't even trust myself in the classroom. I wanted to learn the business, I wanted to learn how to organize things but I was a bad manager because all my staff were older than me. There was a huge learning curve there, I was really bad at telling people what to do.

There was some 'imposter syndrome' going on because, who was I? What did I know?

I was also surprised that people didn't care about my credentials. They would come, if they liked the feel of the studio, and if they liked me, they would stay. I found very quickly that I was selling myself and my values and nobody asked about my degree or if I was a certified dance teacher or if any of my teachers were and I thought that was weird.

I really capitalized on that over the years and realized that I can hire and train amazing young teachers, that don't necessarily come to me with the greatest resumes versus paying $50 an hour to a highly accredited teacher who may have lost touch.

WHAT ARE THREE THINGS THAT YOUR STUDIO DOES BETTER THAN ANYONE ELSE?

First is building community. Like I said, people didn't care about credentials, so realizing that they had to care about finding a home was important. As we got bigger and bigger, I realized that I couldn't be the face of the studio for every single person. So really defining the higher admin structure so that each department had their own director has been the answer.

Each of our departments has anywhere from 100 to 300 children and each one of those departments have their own 'me'. They are a tight community, they feel like it's a small studio within a big studio, and they can benefit from having all of the benefits of a large studio without feeling lost in the crowd, or feeling like they are just a number.

Most of my staff knows every child's name in their department and they could see them in the grocery store and be able to talk to them. Even if they are not in our competitive program, dancers still have things to look forward to every year. They still have a daddy-daughter dance, they still have parades, they still have lock-ins, and they still have all of those little extras that make them have friends at the studio. When our customers are deciding which activity to drop, they are going to drop soccer and not dance because their friends are made at dance.

Secondly, we run the studio like a business and not a hobby. We have hundreds of local studios in our area, and the comments that I hear most often with people switching to our studio or coming and inquiring, is that their previous studio is much-loved but so disorganized.

We have our calendar out so far in advance and are never changing things last minute. Parents really, really appreciate it, and it sets us apart a lot in our area.

The third thing we do really well is teaching to the whole child and not just the dancer. We are always reminding them of core values, and we have a really strong mentorship program at the studio that feeds into our assistant program. The parents see it from even the recreational level. We're teaching them about teamwork and leadership and we're infusing it into their lessons.

There is a bigger picture at play because we all know that 99% of our children are not going on to be professional dancers, so while we have them, I want to make sure that we're teaching them life skills.

YOU ARE A BIT OF A DELEGATION GODDESS – WHAT IS YOUR ADVICE TO STUDIO OWNERS WHO MAY NOT FEEL COMFORTABLE OR CONFIDENT IN DELEGATING IMPORTANT TASKS IN THEIR BUSINESS?

Where people go wrong is they are outsourcing things, rather than actually truly delegating. And those are very different. If you give somebody a list of things to do, you're really just outsourcing them. You're saying, "Do this, check off the list and give it back to me." But you're still managing that, and that energy is what's exhausting you.

To truly delegate something, your staff has to be empowered to make decisions without you. They need to be able to run things and move things forward and do things without you saying, "Hey, did you order the programs? Did you order the t-shirts?" All of that should be part of their job description and they should know how to do that without needing you entirely.

If you're not giving your staff the tools, and some responsibility and vision of their own, then you're still bearing the burden of all of those tasks. Some of the things that we did early on to allow my directors to be empowered to do that is, they helped come up with the mission statement and our brand promise.

They know where decisions come from, how I would make a decision, if it falls within the mission statement and also within our brand promise, then the answer should be obvious.

The next step is really taking a year to train people to let them do it. Let them make a mistake, let them come back and ask you what you would have done differently, and staying hyper focused on that process. Now my departments run themselves. We have a poster in the office that says, "Departments make decisions" so they remember that I will support their decision, whatever they decide. You have to be able to do that, so you have to let go of a little bit of control.

If I disagree with a decision, we'll talk about it and say, "Next time I prefer you do this." But if they don't make mistakes, they don't understand why things are the way they are and I have to let them go through that same process that I went through when I was young. I didn't glean all of this knowledge perfectly the first time and that makes a huge difference.

I can't even believe how well things run now without having to even involve me. Registration happens, and recital will happen whether I'm there or not. It's great.

YOU HAVE A NUMBER OF THRIVING REVENUE STREAMS WITHIN YOUR STUDIO, INCLUDING DANCE PHOTOGRAPHY. WHAT PROCESSES HAVE SUPPORTED THESE NON-DANCE PROFIT CENTERS IN YOUR BUSINESS?

This also ties into the delegation process. For example, it's recital season right now and there's no way I could dedicate weeks of my time to work on new projects, if I were still doing all recital things like cutting music and ordering costumes and writing programs. So step one: I had all that taken care of to give me the time.

The photography initially stemmed from frustration – which I've heard from so many other studio owners – that they are spending a week in the studio, they are exhausted from posing children, they are exhausted from being there and dealing with the parents on photo day. Worse than that, their revenue is going right out the door to somebody who doesn't seem to care or is too expensive and takes too long. Or sometimes the quality of the pictures are bad. The complaints are so varied when it comes to that area of the business.

I shared all those same frustrations and I also had my first son at the time and realized how expensive pictures were going to be for me, as a mom. So right then and there I thought, *You know what? Let's just see if we can do this.*

I bought the equipment, and at first it was all trial and error because there wasn't a YouTube video for everything. It wasn't hard to get started, because people were already buying amateur pictures. This time they were buying my amateur pictures instead. I was making the revenue from it to quickly and easily pay back all the equipment that very first year, and I only did it for my competitive children because they know me so well and were a wonderful test group to get started.

From that point, year after year, I just tweaked the system. I eventually added my Posing Guide, that ensures that the poses are different for every child, every year, which in turn increases your revenue and takes all of the stress out of picture week because that way you don't have to think at all. It's just all right there for you and then anyone else can do the posing of the dancers for you.

I've logged all of my hours for editing for another studio this year and it was about 15 hours worth of work editing and compiling and ordering, and we easily hit $12,000 in revenue. Right before summer to have that extra boost of income is amazing, and it's not hard work.

WHAT ADVICE CAN YOU GIVE OTHER STUDIO OWNERS WHO MAY BE LOOKING TO INNOVATE AND EXPAND INTO NEW PROJECTS AND REVENUE STREAMS?

Try things but don't be afraid for it not to work. We've tried a million things over the years. We've had an adult program, we've had a childrens' Zumba program, we've tried cheerleading. We've had different programs throughout the years and I would say, first and foremost, have a good handle on what you are already doing. If you feel frantic and scrambling already, don't add anything new. Then once things settle, and you're comfortable with what you have you can explore your ideas more effectively.

And don't ever react with a new program. That's another thing that I've done. A mistake I've made in the past is if a couple of adults for example enquire about a tap class, there's a knee-jerk compulsion to say, "Okay, let's put a tap class together!"

Make sure that you're being profitable or that you have room to grow, and if you do it as a very clear system, an analyzed system, then you'll either know that it worked or it didn't work and you'll know whether or not to keep it. One thing I've definitely learned is that some things work so well for some people and don't work at all for others.

It might be your market or just your personality. Photography worked so well for me because I actually enjoy taking pictures. If you have absolutely no interest in it and it doesn't intrigue you at all, then no, it might not work because you're not going to have any passion for it. You're not going to be excited about it, so don't try to fit a square peg into a round hole. I delegate my birthday parties, for example because it's not what I'm passionate about.

CAN YOU TELL US ABOUT THE BIG MOMENTS IN BUSINESS THAT HAVE REALLY DEFINED YOUR PATH AS A STUDIO OWNER?

When I was younger I had a little college car. It was a tiny little Toyota that died, and when it was time to get a new car, the studio was doing great. My dad's advice was, "You should get a BMW or you should get a Mercedes, you need to show people that you're successful."

And in my mind, I kept thinking, *If I show people that I'm successful, they are going to think I'm charging too much and they are going to think that if only I gave them a cut on tuition, that I wouldn't be able to buy that car.* So I ultimately did not buy a BMW or Mercedes, I bought a little SUV that I felt was the 'right level' of reasonable for what I was charging.

I was having that conversation with somebody who said to me, "If you were having heart surgery and you drove up to your doctor's office and they were driving a little Toyota, would you think very highly of that heart surgeon? Or would you prefer to see your heart surgeon driving the top of the line Mercedes?"

It just hit me. People want to know that I'm good at this, they want to know that they are investing in someone who knows what they are doing and that they are just as proud of me as they would be if I were driving a really nice car.

My second big 'a-ha' moment is now immortalized as a sign in our office, that says, "Do what you want, someone's always going to complain." That has been eye opening to me because I'm always a pleaser. I'm always doing surveys to find 'What's the majority?' I want to make sure the majority is happy.

One year we couldn't decide whether to have a particular rehearsal late at night, or on the weekend so we put a survey out, and the outcome was literally 50/50. No matter which one we choose, half the people are going to be mad at us.

There was another example around the same time, where we had an event at the studio. I don't normally attend every event, but my children were going to this one and so I figured I'd go. I was having so much fun – we were all covered in shaving foam and water, and I was just loving hanging out with my children. One of the moms came to pick up her child and looked at me in the most irritated way and asked, "Don't you have people for this? What are you doing here?"

I thought everyone would think it was so cool that I was there, but the way she looked at it felt like: you are better than this, what are you doing?

Those things all in a short period of time hit me. No matter what I do, there will always be someone who doesn't like it, or doesn't think it's the 'right' way to do things. Looking back to the family event, I could have not been there and half the people would have been impressed that

I have a staff that takes care of those things. Or I could have been there and had half the people think that I shouldn't be, and half the people think that it was great that I took the time to be with the children. Really, you can't please everyone so do what you want, people are always going to complain.

WHAT DO YOU THINK MIGHT BE HOLDING A LOT OF STUDIO OWNERS BACK FROM REACHING THEIR FULL POTENTIAL IN BUSINESS?

A big problem is not knowing that there are resources out there to help them. Not knowing where to find them, not knowing that they exist, thinking that they are all alone and they have to figure it out themselves. Even just watching the free Facebook support groups and realizing the questions being asked are so different from the questions that are asked in the Dance Studio Owners Inner Circle. They are so elementary to me because that's all covered in our calls and in our coaching time.

Fear is another big one. Whether it's fear of success, fear of failure, fear of the unknown, it manifests in excuses. Excuses for not having enough time, excuses for not having enough money, excuses that students aren't coming through the door. If people could hear that and hear themselves and realize that they are making excuses and there's a way around it, that would be the most profound change in a lot of studio owners that I recognize.

WHAT ARE YOUR FAVORITE STUDENT ATTRACTION STRATEGIES?

This sounds so basic, but Facebook ads have been life changing. Doing them well, continuing to learn and follow changes means that ours have become like clockwork. We put an ad out for X number of dollars, we know exactly how many leads we're going to get, we know exactly how many students we're going to get. Our Inner Circle coach Tracy Morgan has been so helpful in all of that, so definitely Facebook ads but taking the time to learn properly and do them well.

YOU ARE MARRIED WITH FOUR YOUNG BOYS – WHAT DOES STUDIO CEO LIFE LOOK LIKE FOR YOUR FAMILY?

It looks like lots of caffeine! More seriously, it's about remembering that I'm building a business for my family, so never seeing my family would completely defeat that purpose. We need to really be strict with our calendar and making sure that we do account for family time. I have found more often than not, parents at the studio appreciate me saying, "No, it's family time, I've got something with my son, I've got to go." They get it. They have families so they are never going to make you feel bad for that.

And that's a lesson that I had to learn along the way. I remember when I felt guilty telling my dance families that I was having my second or third baby, and now they applaud me when I leave and I go to one of my childrens soccer games.

In order to do that comfortably, again it is about truly delegating and giving your staff the room to make decisions without you, and give them the support that you're not going to be mad if they make the wrong decision. That's when they are going to call you on a Sunday and ask you questions, that they could easily have handled by themselves. It's when they don't feel that they don't have the support they need to do that.

At our recent Inner Circle retreat in Las Vegas, Adrienne Dorison talked about the three reasons why your staff can't make decisions:

1. They don't have the information
2. They don't have the permission
3. They are afraid they are going to get in trouble

If you can eliminate those three things, you are golden. We spent a couple of months diving into just those three things. Making sure that the information is accessible to them, and any time someone asks me a question now I say, "Why can't you answer this?" And then we go fix it. I also need to reiterate constantly that they can answer it slightly wrong, but will learn from it and then answer it right the next time.

The final thing that allows me to really spend quality time with my family without worrying about the business is by not sweating the small stuff. I watch so many studio owners lose their minds about a kid who won't gel their bangs back for the recital, or spending $15,000 on a digital backdrop for their recital because it has to be the most amazing thing in the world.

It doesn't matter – what you do in the classroom every single week matters so much more than a ridiculously prop-infused recital at the end of the year, or worrying about a child in the wrong tights or the wrong shoes.

Just let it go. The amount of stress that studio owners put on themselves, is a large portion of the exhaustion, the lack of family time and the inability to grow. If you're upset and worried about your 20 children being perfect, you're not going to be okay with 1,000 children not being perfect. You're going to lose it. Make sure that you have certain things that are your priorities but really don't sweat the small stuff.

I am such a fan of how this husband and wife team approach their studio from a great business mindset while simultaneously delivering an extraordinary customer experience to every single one of their 700+ customers. Their tips and experiences in running a thriving dance studio for almost 20 years could almost be a book of its own.

Amanda and Nathan Barr are the owners of Dance Sensations, the Illawarra's best-known dance studio and one of the largest schools in Australia.

Amanda was inspired to open her studio at just 16 years old and has since grown it into a thriving business with an annual turnover exceeding seven figures. In 2015, Amanda's husband Nathan joined Dance Sensations full-time as they expanded into their second location. Nathan's holds a degree in Mathematics

and Finance, bringing his experience as an accountant, software analyst and high school maths teacher to the business. Nathan also runs a school tutoring business within the dance studio.

By establishing a strong culture and relying on the right practices and systems, Amanda and Nathan have built not just a successful dance school but an award-winning small business. Amanda was also named Business Person of the Year at the 2018 South Coast & Illawarra Business Awards.

Outside of the studio, Amanda and Nathan love spending time with their young family, especially swimming at the Minnamurra River with their three daughters, Azaliah, Gigi and Sassy.

Check out Amanda and Nathan's latest studio news at dancesensations.com.au

Chapter Two

BUILDING YOUR MILLION DOLLAR STUDIO: AMANDA & NATHAN BARR

Dance Sensations

WHAT WAS IT LIKE TO OPEN UP A DANCE STUDIO AT ONLY 16 YEARS OF AGE, AMANDA?

Amanda: I'd always dreamed of being a studio owner, and I also had a bit of a different upbringing to a lot of studio owners in that my parents were in small business and I always knew that I wanted to run my own business from a very young age. They always taught me about their businesses from as long as I can remember, and they used to have conversations about their businesses around the dinner table so that I knew what was going on and I always was exposed to that kind of world.

So I opened the studio in 2001 with the help of my mom. Obviously being 16, I hadn't had a lot of professional dance experience or anything, but I already knew that I was made to be a dance teacher and had started teaching very early at the age of 13.

We bought an existing studio that had about 20 students, and mom and I ran it for two or three years together before I bought it off her. We had one location and got to about 550 students at the one location, then in 2012 we opened our second location and Nathan – my husband – came on board as a full-time staff member.

Today we have about 750 children and run about 200 classes a week with 25 staff.

WHAT IS YOUR 'WHY', AND HAS THIS CHANGED SINCE RUNNING YOUR STUDIO FOR 18 YEARS?

Amanda: I guess my why has changed over time. Originally it was teaching, to share my passion of dance. I felt like the community needed a dance studio and I wanted other people to experience something that was always so special and such a big part of my life.

Now my why is more having my life by design, and being able to choose how my studio runs, how the culture runs. I get to surround myself with the people that I want to surround myself with. I get to choose how much time or what sort of hours I put into work. And I get to choose how I want to live.

Our why inside the studio has also become more personal. Now we talk about how we want to make it a special place and that children can make memories and it's not always about creating the most amazing dancer or someone with the most amazing technique, but allowing children to have that special place that they feel like a second home.

YOU HAVE THREE YOUNG DAUGHTERS – HOW DID THINGS CHANGE FOR YOU AND THE BUSINESS WHEN THEY WERE BORN?

Amanda: It changed most after our second daughter was born to be honest when it felt like more of a significant change to our whole dynamic. As you get older and family becomes more of a priority, you realize that it's not all about work and profit. It's about more than that. It's about your lifestyle as well.

WHO ARE YOUR BIGGEST BUSINESS INSPIRATIONS AND WHY?

Amanda: 100% my mom is my role model. My parents have always owned lots of businesses together, but mom specifically has quite a lot herself. She has always been the hardest worker and has success from that, and she's taught me a lot about business. I still go to them for advice all the time on how we're running our business.

She said to me recently that she is a big believer in leading by example to her staff and her team. And even though that's not something that should be happening all the time for a CEO, if something needs to be done she gets in there and she does it with her team. She works harder than anybody else in a business and that's why she's had success. And as a business owner that's what you need to do.

Another one of the biggest things she's taught me as well are some amazing customer service lessons. That is something we brought to our studio a lot earlier than a lot of other studios did who just didn't have it on their radar as the consumer climate changed and evolved.

NATHAN, HOW HAS YOUR PAST EXPERIENCE INFLUENCED THE OPERATIONS OF YOUR STUDIO?

Nathan: In college, I was a Subway™ Sandwich Artist, and like any fast food outlet you get exposed to the importance of systems. When I made a sub I had to cut the bread exactly this way, and I had to put six slices of tomato exactly. You couldn't just turn up and think, *How am I going to make it today?*

The importance of those systems, so that the customer gets the same level of product or service every single time, is something we really prioritize in the studio.

I have a mathematics and finance degree and have worked as an accountant, which of course helps with the financial side of the studio. I've also had experience as a software analyst which has helped me effectively integrate and manage the wide range of IT systems that we have in the studio.

From working in a high school with a teaching background, it does help me to empathize with our staff. My biggest take away from that was making sure that you're valuing the good of your staff as well, and using the collective knowledge of your staff to help your business improve.

HOW HAVE YOU ADAPTED TO CHANGED ATTITUDES AND EXPECTATIONS FROM YOUR CUSTOMERS OVER THE YEARS?

Amanda: Parents' expectations have grown exponentially, especially over the last eight years or so. And I think that's because the studio owners across the board do set a high bar. Compared to a lot of other children's sports, we set a much higher bar in terms of customer service and organization and a professional business model. And as you keep improving that, that the parent's expectations keep getting higher.

That's applicable in customer service, but also in terms of what their children are being taught in class. Social media has played a huge role in that because they see the Instagram famous dancers and don't always see what goes on behind the scenes of that amazing pirouette. It's important that we do our best to educate parents that things aren't always what they seem and not every child can do what that specific dancer does, or appears to be doing.

WHAT QUALITIES SET YOUR STUDIO APART?

Amanda: We've always offered a really high level of customer service. We have dedicated a very large admin team, including people that welcome everyone at the door, make sure that the students are settled and help everyone through that process. We have staff that float in our reception, because we have quite a large reception, and a lot of children.

One of the biggest compliments I've ever got from someone that's come to our concert and said that they can't tell apart our recreational dancers to our competition dancers, because we work so hard on making sure all the dancers are given equal opportunities and that everyone is special in our studio. Whereas I feel that some studios focus on their competition dancers and don't give as much thought in their concert or their recital to the recreational ones. It's super important to us, and we have a huge recreational stream because we make sure that everyone feels special and unique.

We try to do lots of little special touches for the dancers and for the parents throughout the year that makes their time with us special, and things that they will remember for years to come.

Our studio culture's really ingrained and that sets us apart. We're so lucky, at the moment we only have three or four of our staff that aren't ex-students of ours and because of that they remember what it was like.

They then build on our culture and expand it even more, and they don't need to be taught it. A lot of them have been with our studio for the whole 19 years.

It's very important to them to pass that on to the other students. That really makes our studio unique to have that culture. We talk about how it's a family and it really does highlight that when so many of our students and our teachers have been with us for such a long period of time.

IF I WAS A NEW STUDENT COMING TO YOUR STUDIO, WHAT WOULD MY FIRST DAY LOOK LIKE?

Amanda: We first have an enrollment coordinator who talks through everything with the parents, answers the emails or the phone call, Facebook message, or whatever it is, and their job is to build a strong relationship with you before you even come into the studio so you know exactly what to expect when you come in.

We then have one of our front desk staff who is going to greet you when you come to the class. We usually have a junior that will help you go to your classroom and get settled in your class. That may mean sitting with them when you first meet the teacher, or you may need an extra person to stay in the class holding your hand, that's what happens. Whatever you need, we will go there.

After the class both our front desk staff and the teacher will give some feedback on how the lesson went. Our enrollment co-ordinator then touches base again the following day to confirm the enrollment.

YOU BOTH WORK TOGETHER FULL-TIME IN THE STUDIO – CAN YOU DESCRIBE THAT WORKING RELATIONSHIP?

Amanda: I personally operate on instinct a lot. There's way too much of an opportunity for people to overthink things and over complicate it. And sometimes there's too much information and sometimes you should just go with the gut. I am learning and always growing as well. I know that everyone makes mistakes – myself included – and that's okay. It's how you handle those mistakes and what you do to fix them and move on.

Nathan deals with more of the finances of the business and runs our separate tutoring business, and I do more of the staff and the day-to-day running of the studio, as well as the events and the dance side.

WHY DO YOUR STUDENTS STAY WITH YOU FOR SO LONG?

Amanda: We work on making sure every child feels special in the class and that's something that my teachers are all phenomenal at doing. They work really hard on making sure they check in with children. If they have a feeling that a child might be losing interest or if there's something wrong or something going on, they make sure that either they touch base with a parent or they get one of our admin team to call and check in on that child.

Our events are really special, and they are a huge retention tool for us. We have two main recitals a year and run them in different ways, so that different people get to enjoy different aspects of them no matter what their style is. We have huge retention because they love that variety.

We also work really hard on great customer service, making sure our admin team know everybody's name. They walk in and they greet them by name and say, "Hi, little Suzy. I love your bow today! How was your school disco the other night?" We try to remember personal things about that child or the family or the parent, to try and make it a place that they feel super comfortable and at home.

WHAT HAS BEEN THE BIGGEST CHALLENGE FOR YOU SO FAR IN YOUR STUDIO JOURNEY?

Amanda: Learning to scale the business has definitely been one of the biggest challenges and lessons so far. All of a sudden it just got very big. We had three studios and 500 children, but once we had the two locations and we got towards the 750 mark, it started to become very challenging. It was very different trying to stay on top of every child and keeping all of our notes and communication working efficiently.

Things started to turn around when I started letting go and trusting my systems. It's not like we didn't have the systems in place, our staff are awesome. It's just me letting go of it and not needing to know every single thing that was going on.

One of our biggest lessons was that it's important to grow the right way. We had two locations and we have since closed one because we had a big growth in student numbers and grew our revenue to seven figures, our expenses also hit the seven figure mark! And so our profit didn't grow. It was exactly the same, but it was a lot more work.

Nathan: Absolutely! There are different ways to grow. Bigger isn't always better because at the end of the day, as a business, we need to focus on the profit as well.

Another thing that we talked about was trusting culture. That our culture is so deeply ingrained in all of our staff, that we needed to trust that more and that they were going to give the answer that they knew Amanda would give when we set those systems in place for Amanda to step back from the day-to-day.

WHAT ADVICE WOULD YOU GIVE YOURSELF IF YOU COULD GO BACK IN TIME AND HAVE A CHAT WITH 16-YEAR OLD AMANDA AND NATHAN?

Amanda: It's a marathon and not a sprint. And that things take time. It takes time to develop the dancers you want, the culture you want, the systems you want, and those things come in time. You have to have a thick skin and learn that fast and not take things personally all the time. Because it's not usually personal.

It's also important to remember that in business there will always be peaks and valleys; things go up and down and that's okay. To have those high highs sometimes you've got to have a low to get there and so many times it makes those highs sweeter when you know you've worked for them and had a bit of a hard time in between.

I invited our next successful studio owner to be a part of Dance Studio Secrets because I absolutely love the energy that she brings to every project. She has a phenomenal passion and spirit about everything she does, and is one of those people with the unique ability to light up a room just by walking through the doors. Cara not only gets the phenomenal work done, she also makes everybody around her feel special.

Cara Poppitt is the CEO of Soul Connexion in Calgary, Canada.

As a dancer Cara trained in New York and LA for several seasons, danced professionally in Mexico and the Dominican Republic and brought her unique hip hop and Latin style to Calgary. Her passionate pursuit led her to many opportunities; from performing overseas, to television roles, to commercials, movies and concerts.

Cara completed a combined degree from the University of Calgary in Business and Psychology with a focus in health psychology. Cara was previously Western Canada's Student Entrepreneur for 2005 and a recipient of Global Television's Woman of Vision for Arts and Culture in 2009.

Cara expands beyond the studio walls to offer dance, yoga and fitness programs to the public and catholic school district boards. She continues to volunteer her time with the business school and loves working with female entrepreneurs.

Aside from the studio, she has three amazing children that teach her new things every day, as well as a wonderful husband.

Check out Cara's latest studio news at soulconnexion.ca

Chapter Three

TURNING DREAMS INTO ACTION: CARA POPPITT

Soul Connexion Ltd.

WHAT SURPRISED YOU THE MOST IN YOUR FIRST YEAR OF RUNNING THE BUSINESS?

What surprised me the most was the magnitude of things the studio owner is responsible for. If I could do it again, I would really try to get more ON the business rather than IN the business.

When I first opened I had a business plan and tried to execute it as closely as possible. So, I did a lot of planning first (which was great!) but what surprised me was just how much you're in the business all the time. It's very encompassing and time consuming – you just can't get away from it.

I would wake up, open the studio at 6:00 am, and teach a morning bootcamp class. I worked admin at the front desk between teaching classes all day. I was busy daily from 6:00 am – 9:00 pm just to get the studio up and running.

If I were to do it again, I would try to take out a larger loan, so I could hire more help. It's always so tight when you start a business and you take out so much risk.

HOW DO YOU DEBRIEF WITH YOUR TEAM AFTER PROJECTS AND EVENTS SO YOU CAN PULL OUT AS MANY LESSONS AS POSSIBLE FOR THE FUTURE?

After anything that's brand new that we execute on – for example, showcases, photo day, new training – we put time aside to talk right away. If it's recital, we're still at the venue while it's fresh in our head.

I've also learned that it can be really hard for people because they are like "Oh my gosh, I just worked my butt off and now you're telling me what we did wrong?" So, what I like to do is to talk about the really good things first. Then we ask, "What would take it to the next level?" That's usually how I frame it. Then we go over any issues that happened and what we could do differently, then we document it right there because you're just going to forget in two weeks if you wait.

And your emotions are quite high after a big event, it also brings the team together.

I am transparent in letting my team know that they are going to have the opportunity to give and receive feedback. It's important to me that they understand the importance of feedback, if we want to grow and evolve. I let them know that if they are not okay with feedback, it's going to be very uncomfortable working here.

WHAT PROJECTS THAT YOU'RE WORKING ON NOW ARE YOU MOST EXCITED ABOUT?

Part of what makes me tick is the creative element. I love coming up with an idea, and then finding a plan and getting people to help me with the plan. That brings me joy, and it fuels my heart and my soul, and then it gives me more inspiration for other things. For example, we have a new mascot, Soulina, who has been so much fun to work with and now we are ready to expand with that.

Soulina needs to go to schools, and she needs to teach children how to dance. It's those new, creative projects that really fill my cup.

I'm also working on a teacher manual for my teachers. We have a handbook, admin manuals, studio manuals, show handbook, welcome orientation, community events – you get the picture! Everything that I do has been documented for the last eight years. It's been such a valuable asset in ensuring the quality and expectations in the studio are consistent and clear, and that our staff have everything they need to do an exceptional job.

The focus of my new teacher manual is skills that will help my staff excel. It will include training on how to connect with parents, how to wow families at viewing week, how to speak with confidence, etc. All these skills are crucial as a dance teacher and need to be taught.

I just completed a Fine Arts Club Curriculum for preschool aged children, available for sale complete with lesson plans, crafts, playlists, policies, manuals, etc exclusively for dance studios. I love working on projects that allow me to be creative and make an impact.

WHAT DO YOU THINK ARE THE MOST IMPORTANT QUALITIES IN A DANCE TEACHER?

I really believe that people come to a class and they keep coming back, because of the way the teacher makes them feel. And I believe that it's about connecting, so it's about their body language, it's their energy, it's how they look, it's how they talk, it's how they make eye contact, it's how they smile, it's paying attention to the little things.

I hire different personalities, but I hire people that can connect, people that are self-aware, people that can ask good, intelligent questions, who can actively listen to people and give them feedback, because as a teacher you have to be able to analyze the room really quickly, manage energy, and you need to stop negativity before it can happen.

They have to be aware of people and become experts of people. The longer you teach the more effective you become. But there's also a huge component of education, about teaching different learning styles. A lot of people don't even know the different learning styles or different communication styles.

If I'm saying something but the child still not doing it, I need to demonstrate, or I need to go and physically touch their leg, or I need to ask them a question, or get them to repeat it. There are different ways children will retain information, same with adults. Teachers that are really successful with adults are the ones that are comfortable within their own skin, and they give people permission to be themselves too. So, for me, the number one thing I look for is, yes they have to be a great dance teacher, they have to be a good dancer, but they need to be able to connect with people.

I do a class assessment with all my teachers once or twice a year.

So, I go into their class, I watch the entire class, I take a ton of notes. What I've learned is that you can't just email this to them and they are going to read it and understand it. You've got to sit down and take half an hour and debrief and ask questions like, "How did you feel when this happened?" Or, "I noticed this happened with this student, did you think it was effective?" And sometimes when they ask question and give answers, they have their own self-awareness.

One of my topics for the manual is going to be positive redirection, so when people aren't doing what you want them to do, how can you redirect them in a positive way. If a child has a negative experience, where you have hurt their spirit or self-confidence, it's hard to gain that back. And the best gift we can give our children is the gift of confidence, and parents are always looking for that. Whether we're the most technical or highly competitive, they also look for those life skills, so we blend those in with our teaching method, with the parties we hold, and with our communication to our parents.

It has to be set from the teachers, they need to be able to connect. Our administrators need to be able to connect, and we need to be able to flow. I do a teacher retreat at the beginning of every year, I do two teacher parties too, where we just get together. Once a month we meet for pleasure, I teach them our choreography for our 'teacher dance' and we usually hang out after. We do a pedicure party at the end of the year, and I take a lot of moments where I can build them up and fuel them. Because the more you pour into them, the more they pour into their students, and the more the studio thrives.

HOW HAVE YOU BEEN ABLE TO MAINTAIN AND GROW A THRIVING ADULT COMPONENT IN YOUR STUDIO?

We're a dance-yoga-fitness studio, so we run adult programs as well. When I first opened, we had four studio rooms, so I wanted to just have as many classes going on as possible. Our market is quite saturated with different yoga and fitness studios, so I'm always trying to be innovative and create new things. So we run Zumba bootcamps, kickboxing, yoga, etc.

We run a lot of classes when the children can't come here, so first thing in the morning, we'll do 9:00 am until noon classes, we'll do 8:00 pm classes, and then weekends as well. I add those classes in wherever I have time space. Offering a wide spread of programs is very, very smart. So, when the market changes you're adapting, and you're evolving, and you're never stuck and you're never shrinking. You're always maintaining and growing.

We also make sure that we are making it really easy for them. We run 12-week programs, or small programs, I don't think a lot of adults want to commit to a full year program. We attract more recreational users, so they are the moms who want to do yoga once a week, or they work out three times a week, but they are not hardcore taking two classes a day. That's not our market. And we make people feel very comfortable, so we do end up getting a lot of beginners, especially for yoga. It's not intimidating and we create the vibe and the ambiance, but it's also not a traditional yoga studio, where it's super quiet and peaceful.

WHAT ARE SOME OF THE BIGGEST WINS YOU'VE ACHIEVED IN YOUR BUSINESS?

Hitting our ten years is significant because a lot of businesses fail after five years. A lot of the area around us, there's studios popping up, and there's also a lot of studios closing down. So growing and really being able to grow your programs, grow your people, grow your offerings, grow your value, is a really big accomplishment for me.

Also just reflecting on a personal level, I have had three children, so being able to start a business, the next year have your first child, and then have two more children, and keep going, is crazy! When you find what you're passionate about, and you have energy, you find ways to make it happen.

I was nominated for Woman of Vision in 2007 when I opened. It was the very large award on global television, so that was nice to be recognized. Every time you get nominated for an award it's nice, because you're like, "Oh, I do make a difference in the community."

WHAT ARE SOME OF THE BOUNDARIES THAT YOU'VE PUT IN PLACE TO MAKE WORK AND HOME LIFE HARMONIOUS?

With any business owner, regardless of the industry, when you start you are so consumed. You're in the washroom checking your phone, before you go to bed, you're sleeping with your phone. It's just too much of a connection. When I see all these different people run their successful businesses, the older they got, the more space they put between themselves and their business. They add more boundaries.

I'm quite good at turning my phone off now, I would recommend any business owner to be strategic with when you're going to check email, when you're going to work, and then be done. At the beginning you must be more connected, because you really want to serve the market, and get into the market.

But as you get more experience, it's important that you have a life too.

YOU HAVE A BUSINESS DEGREE AND A PSYCHOLOGY DEGREE. HOW HAS YOUR EDUCATIONAL BACKGROUND SERVED YOU IN RUNNING YOUR STUDIO?

I went to university for a degree in business, majoring in marketing. And then I also did a degree in psychology. There was an article written on me when I was in university, it said, "The psychology of dance business." Because to me, business is about connecting with people. If you can connect to people you can run a really solid business, but if you can't connect to people, how are you going to offer your services, or how are you going to do anything?

I used to work for a venture capital firm before I had the studio. And I had courses on selling, connecting with people, and matching and mirroring styles. I went into opening the studio with more of a plan than other people may have.

Understanding people and different personality types is huge. This is true in any business, especially dance, because we're feeling-type people, we feel energy.

I love traveling, and when you travel and when you explore you learn new things. And you can apply that back into your business or your life. Sometimes when you have complete breaks from your business, you get more fuel and more fire, and the best ideas will come to you. Taking yoga training has helped me too, so everything I've done keeps building me.

HOW DO YOU TURN YOUR STUDENTS INTO RAVING, REFERRING FANS?

It's all about the experience. Everything falls into that. How do you make them feel, how do you connect to them, how do you encourage them, how do you inspire them? Our year end shows are done differently, so we do slide shows, when they walk in there's pictures from the whole year. It's reinforcing our culture and showcasing who we are. And children love seeing pictures of themselves! It's in all of the little things, the little subtleties.

Although we are big picture thinkers, we do not skip out on the small details. It's our way to show our appreciation to our clients, who in turn, keep coming back because we make them feel good.

We host a Christmas party (complete with a dancing Santa) and host team building events and appreciation parties.

We do small things with great love. It's all in the delivery, our tone, our communication, and our vibe.

Of all the studio owners I work with, my next Dance Studio Secrets guest has a consistent ability to focus and implement on her vision that stands out. When Heather has a goal she maps out a project plan, gets the resources she needs and is laser focused on executing on that project to achieve her results. Heather is the definition of a Dance Studio CEO.

Heather Wrubel is the CEO of Bowman Dance Company & School in Pennsylvania, USA. Heather opened her doors in 2010 with the goal of providing a quality dance educational facility that would engage students in the performing arts.

She holds a Bachelor of Fine Arts in Dance Education with Distinguished Honors from the University of the Arts in Philadelphia, graduating in 2000. Heather has trained in Germany at the Senden Schule of Musik and the Stuttgart Ballet. Prior to founding Bowman Dance Company & School, Heather was the Dean of the dance department of Gadsden Elementary Fine and Performing Arts School in Savannah, Georgia.

She has performed Paul Taylor's *Esplanade* in the 2000 Feet Festival in Philadelphia. At the young age of 12 Heather worked with a touring company performing the *Nutcracker* ballet throughout southern Bavaria, Germany. Heather is still performing today with Blind Faith Project in Philadelphia.

She is married and lives with her husband and two children in Sounderon, Pennsylvania. She loves to watch her son play baseball and spend time on the lake with her family.

Check out Heather's latest studio news at bowmandance.com

Chapter Four

BECOMING THE STUDIO CEO: HEATHER WRUBEL

Bowman Dance Company & School

HOW DID YOU GET STARTED IN BUSINESS AS A DANCE STUDIO OWNER?

I started my studio like most studio owners. I grew up dancing, loved dancing, went to school for dancing, performed, had a performance career, and decided that the passion and love for dance was something I wanted to share with the community and with young people coming up into the industry. So, I decided that I was going to open my studio.

I did not have the money or cash flow to do so, so I left the industry and went into corporate America and worked in property management to fund my dance studio startup.

I did that for about five years before I opened my studio, but it was hard times starting up. And because I hadn't been working in the industry for five years, I didn't really have a student following anymore, so I started from zero.

When I opened my doors in June of 2010, I literally had zero registrations and we built the studio from the ground up.

That first year over the summer, we had 30 students. Then when we opened in September for our first season, we had 78 children who had enrolled. The biggest struggle that I had was that I was still working full-time and trying to run the studio at the same time with a four-year-old at home and a family and all of that.

So it was really time consuming and very stressful, not only on myself, but on my family. And that wasn't something that my family or myself had really thought was going to be such a big problem or such a big issue for us to overcome. The time commitment that I was putting in as a brand new business owner teaching almost every single class and doing all of the admin, finance, marketing, anything and everything that had to do with business.

WHAT STUDENT ATTRACTION STRATEGIES WORKED GREAT FOR YOU IN GETTING YOUR FIRST WAVE OF STUDENTS WHEN YOU WERE STARTING FROM SCRATCH?

The biggest strategy we put in place was getting into the community. We are lucky in my local area. Every single township has a community day either in the spring or in the fall. And even in the spring before it opened, I did every single community day. I had a booth set up with our program information and giveaways.

My mom was with me, and she was a godsend. She's a real estate agent, so marketing is her forte. She hit the streets for me. She went into all the local businesses in and around our community handing out fliers and information and brochures and asking people to come to our open houses.

We also cross-marketed. She took all their marketing material, so honing those partnerships with local businesses early on before I even opened my doors was very, very helpful.

In our local area here, we have a *Clipper Magazine*, which is a coupon book. I put an ad in that coupon book every single month from May through September. Everyone would bring that ad in, so I know that's where a lot of new students came from. So through the community events as well as that *Clipper Magazine* ad where we always had a special offer. Sometimes it was 50% off registration or a three-class free pass to get them to walk in the door with the ad. Most of those clients stayed with us. Out of those first 78 students, we have 60 of them that still dance with us after nine years, which I'm very proud of.

HOW WOULD YOU DESCRIBE YOUR LEADERSHIP STYLE NOW AFTER NINE YEARS, COMPARED WITH WHEN YOU FIRST OPENED YOUR DOORS?

I have a unique leadership style because I have more of a mentorship style. I seek and get a lot of feedback from my employees, my teachers, and my staff and we work together to formulate what works for them and what works for me in moving forward with plans that we're doing.

And I try to get them involved as much as possible in the planning process of what we're doing so they are invested. I really want them to feel like they are a part of what we're doing here because so much of what they do, especially now that I'm not in the studio as much, is really the heartbeat of what happens here.

I want them to understand that what they do is very important and to feel appreciated and understood. So I find myself more as a mentor. Even if something goes wrong and not really the way I had anticipated, it's more of an attitude of, *How can we learn from this? How can we make it better? What do we need to do differently to make this more efficient and smoother for our clients or for you or for us as a school on a whole?*

But this wasn't always the case.

When I first opened and the studio was my baby that I had started from the ground up, I took everything very personally at first. When a student dropped or a teacher left or something didn't go just right, I took it very personally. I've since found that it has nothing to do with me – it has to do with everything else. A student leaves for many reasons, not because I did something wrong necessarily. It could be just because they are interested in theater now or their family has moved out of our location or any number of reasons. So, I now definitely don't take things as personally as I used to like I did when we first started.

And I always say everything happens for a reason. When we are working through any conflict within the studio, I ask, "Why is this happening and what can we do to learn from it to make things better?"

I'm always looking at how we can improve what we do here. And that's one of the things that I always talk about when I'm doing a re-enrollment is we're constantly looking to improve, and these are the things that are coming up for next year that we're looking to improve upon from the program from last year just to get people excited about what's coming. I'm letting them know that we're never really standing still. I'm not the kind of person that just stands still. We're constantly evolving as people. Our students are constantly evolving, so we as a studio have to constantly evolve and grow and develop into what our students and family needs.

WHAT PROCESSES DO YOU FIND WORK BEST FOR YOU WHEN IT COMES TO COMMUNICATIONS WITH YOUR TEACHERS AND OFFICE STAFF?

We use Slack software a lot because we have a lot of different teams. We have a preschool team. We have a school-age team. I have my office team and staff. So, I have different channels to communicate with each one of them differently. I find a lot of times when you overload them with information they don't need, they naturally tune you out or tune out what's happening, and they don't pay attention to what's important. It gets lost. So I find having the separate channels to be able to communicate very specifically with people that need information helps.

We also have monthly meetings for our teaching team and our teachers. We meet once a month to go over events that are coming up, events that have happened, or things that need to be addressed. If there's new information going out, we hash all that out once a month in a 30-minute meeting.

And then with my office team, we meet once a week. We have a weekly huddle just to go through everything, to make sure we're all on the same page in addition to communicating through Slack.

WHAT ARE SOME OF YOUR FAVORITE STRATEGIES THAT YOU'VE IMPLEMENTED IN GROWING YOUR STUDENT NUMBERS SO CONSISTENTLY OVER THE LAST EIGHT YEARS IN BUSINESS?

One of the greatest things that I implemented was our enrollment process. It's the Dance Studio Owners Inner Circle enrollment process that we adopted. We had a process, it just had lots of gaps. And in implementing that along with our software system with Pipedrive, meshing those two together really helped us to seal the deal with a lot of our clients and increased our closing ratio.

We get tons of leads and tons of calls for classes, but there was never any follow-up. Enquiries were on sticky notes and then they got tossed in the trash. And we never knew what happened from one day to the next with someone who had called in about a class.

Formalizing that system was beneficial to us growing and improving on how the customer experience was when they first walked in the door. Being able to treat every single person with the same level of customer service no matter who they are or what they are interested in at the studio was huge for us growing.

As far as our retention, it's really our sense of community, and honing in on what it's like to be a dance community. In our school, we do lots of community events inside and outside of the studio between performances and social events, really getting the entire family involved. We do things including our annual pancake breakfast that we host to announce our end of the year show theme.

Our six main local supermarkets donate $25 gift cards each and that covers all the food that we would buy for the pancake breakfast. And our company parents, which is our competitive team, help out. So we divide and conquer in making the pancakes. We set up our studio into a little diner on a Sunday morning and we just rotate.

We have a slideshow that we put together with all of the end of the year show costumes and those that auditioned for character parts, they get to find out what they have been selected for and whether or not they've made the production cast, and doing the opening and closing dance. We get tons of interest around that, which keeps children all the way through to the end of the year because it happens in October and then the show is in June. Everyone is excited coming in to the season and wanting to stay until the end of the year to finish out that show, which has really been huge in our retention. It's a lot of fun, and the children really enjoy it.

Another thing that we do is have lots of performance opportunities, and we do outside events like going to the zoo and performing at all of our community days.

When I first started, I said that I went to all those community days in our township, and now all our dancers are performing in them. They love it because they love being out in the community and seeing all their friends and talking about what they are doing with us, which is great.

YOU'VE GOT YOUR NO-GAPS ENROLLMENT PROCESS RUNNING EFFECTIVELY, SO ONCE YOU ENROLL A NEW STUDENT HOW DO YOU KEEP THEM?

Our onboarding system from the Inner Circle has been a huge game changer. Last year, it was the first year that we had started in September, I went through and really hashed out our onboarding system for our current students that are coming in and the new students coming in. We separated out both. We had an onboarding for current families that were coming back and an onboarding system for our new families coming in that are going to fit into that email campaign every time we get a new enrollment.

I find that that has been extremely helpful in having families feel welcome and feeling that they know what's going on and that they are a part of something right away – no matter when they join us in the year. They are getting a taste of who I am, who the school is, what we're about, and what we do.

And then it's not just about being with us for one season. We talk about their lifetime journey as a dancer as well as the different paths that their child can take between being in recreational dance program to all the different services that we have, all the events we have coming up. They really get to see the big picture right from the beginning, which has been really, really helpful.

A key in keeping the students with us and having them stay long-term is because we lay that out for them in the onboarding system, that it's not just about taking one class or six classes or being here for three, four, five months. It's about being with us for eight to ten years.

This concept that we have about our dance studio and our dance programs is about being a life journey. Because normally when you get someone that starts dancing, if they really love it and are passionate about it, they stay with it throughout their adulthood most of the time. They'll take adult classes, they'll teach, or they'll do something in the arts or be involved in it in some way. And when we talk about that with new parents – they don't understand that. They think it's a six-week program like what they get at the 'Y'.

And they don't understand the impact that dance can have on their children and what benefits they have for them.

It's one of the reasons why in our re-enrollment packs this year, we introduced a continual enrollment, which means we're assuming you're going to be dancing with us until you tell us that you're not. We're going to be automatically enrolling dancers into next season unless they tell us that they don't want to.

We're not going to be hounding our families every year to re-enroll – we're going to tell them what we recommend. If they don't like it, they can change it, and they can opt-out. But we're past constantly asking whether they are going to come back. We're just assuming they are coming back and putting that time we would have spent on re-enrollment to further evolving the studio and improving the customer journey.

WHAT ADVICE WOULD YOU GIVE TO ANY STUDIO OWNERS WHO MIGHT BE STRUGGLING WITH BALANCING THE DEMANDS OF THE STUDIO AND FAMILY LIFE RIGHT NOW?

One thing that I found early on was that my husband and I were drifting further and further apart because we were on such opposite schedules. He would leave at four in the morning and as he was coming in, I was running out the door.

Or I didn't see him because when I first started, I was working full-time, so we'd leave at about the same time in the morning and I wouldn't see him until the next morning because he would be asleep when I got home. It's like we never really saw each other.

So, we made a plan once a month when we set a date night. And we had a babysitter come in and we had them booked every month. And we made it consistent, so it would be the second Saturday of the month, every month. We knew that this was the day, and this was what we were going to do. Even if we didn't have anything planned, we just ran out the door and grabbed something quick.

It was time knowing that we were going to be together. Very consistent, and it really did help with us communicating and planning our family life.

And also just being adults and being alone and not having all the distractions of children and work and phones and all of that, to kind of just focus on each other. Because without that, we would not be in the same great place we are today.

CAN YOU SHARE ANY BIG LESSONS OR BUSINESS FRAMEWORKS THAT YOU HAVE CARRIED OVER FROM YOUR TIME IN THE CORPORATE WORLD IN TO RUNNING A SUCCESSFUL STUDIO?

In the corporate world I worked in property management, and I was a property manager for a multi-million-dollar property for a huge company here in the suburbs of Philadelphia.

I really did a lot with budgeting and maintaining a budget, dealing with a large staff, and dealing with customer service, maintenance, new prospective residents coming in, maintaining a sales team, the marketing team, all of that. It really did help me understand that process is important.

Coming into owning my own dance studio, I did transfer a lot of those processes into what I do here as far as how we talk on the phone and how we take information from a new, prospective dance student. It's very similar to how we would take information from a new prospective resident.

In the property management industry, how I look at budgeting, how I look at finances, just being able to handle the admin side of things with Google Sheets and spreadsheets and understanding how those work in organizations. All of those things are very important.

And being in corporate America, being able to transfer those skills into my current business helped me to really jumpstart.

Within that first year I started with zero students, we went from 30 to 78.

The next year we had 114.

And from there we just constantly grew. Having that background in implementing systems – even though there were gaps – really did save me a ton of time, effort, and energy, and made it way more efficient than a lot of studio owners coming in that don't have that same experience.

That's why my number one advice for someone coming in new is to make sure that you understand the systems that you need and the systems that you want and really plan them out and implement them from day one because it really does help.

HOW DID YOU EFFECTIVELY TRANSITION FROM TEACHING EVERY CLASS WHEN YOU OPENED, TO NOW TEACHING FOR JUST ONE HOUR A WEEK?

I've been slowly taking myself out for a while. I had my daughter five years ago, so when I found out that I was pregnant with her I knew that my due date was going to be around production season for us.

I knew that I was not going to be able to teach that year because having someone new coming in to teach so close to the end of the year is very hard for young dancers. So, I started out the season that year, I hired four teachers that year, and I completely took myself out of teaching that year 100%.

I was working the front desk only and I would sub from time-to-time if I was able to physically. And that kind of jump started me into moving more into the CEO role because I did a lot more of the admin, a lot more of the planning, a lot more visionary work because I had the time to do it because I was not teaching.

When I had my daughter, I slowly put myself back in because I felt like I needed to, and I loved it and it was my studio and I should be teaching. So, I went back and was teaching about three days a week after I had my daughter. And I found out that it was really difficult to maintain the visionary, growth, planning, structure work that I had been doing while I was pregnant while teaching three days a week.

So the very next year, I cut myself out again, and it took a two year process for me to get to where I am now where I'm only teaching one private lesson a week.

I was so thrilled that our next guest said 'yes' to be featured in Dance Studio Secrets, because her commitment to the growth of her students deserves to be celebrated. Michelle is always looking at ways to be innovative while delivering an unparalleled level of training to help her students grow.

Michelle Hopper Doyle is the CEO of Launch Performing Arts Centre in Queensland, Australia.

As a leader in the Australian dance industry, Michelle has worked extensively in the performing arts for more than 20 years. Her career has seen her work with the world's best directors and choreographers including Baz Luhrmann, George Miller, David Atkins, Kelley Abbey, Wade Robson, The Squared Division, John O'Connell, Jason Coleman and Dein Perry.

With a career spanning over two decades, Michelle secured roles in major stage productions including *Singin' in the Rain* playing the role of Cyd Cherise and Grease Arena Spectacular. She was cast in feature films including *Moulin Rouge, The Great Gatsby, Happy Feet* 1 and 2, *Goddess, The Son of Mask* and performed on screen for multiple prime time events and programs.

She has performed with leading music icons including Kylie Minogue, Jessica Mauboy, Tina Arena, Guy Sebastian, Boyzone, Vanessa Amorosi, The Rogue Traders, Gabriella Cilmi, 30 Seconds to Mars, Cobra Starship, Macy Gray, Dannii Minogue, Adam Lambert, Sheena Easton, Gloria Gaynor, Wynter Gordon, The Veronicas, and Sneaky Sound System.

Michelle lives on the Gold Coast in Australia with her husband and two children.

Check out Michelle's latest studio news at launchpac.com

Chapter Five

TRAINING THE DANCERS OF TOMORROW: MICHELLE HOPPER-DOYLE

Launch Performing Arts Centre

YOU HAVE HAD A HUGE CAREER AS A PERFORMER BOTH BEFORE AND DURING YOUR STUDIO OWNER JOURNEY. CAN YOU TELL US ABOUT SOME OF YOUR CAREER HIGHLIGHTS TO DATE?

I grew up and trained on the Gold Coast with Peter McKinney and Robert Sturrock. Robert Sturrock was a big highlight and influence for me in regards to training because there were no pre-professional courses back then, but he essentially provided that for me.

As a performer I started with jobs that were typical for dancers here on the Gold Coast – I worked as 'Catwoman' at Movie World, and as a dancer at Jupiters Casino which are both real icons locally. I had a great time working on cruise ships for a little while before I came back to the Gold Coast to train with Robert again.

When I was 21 and working for Robert, a movie audition came up that I decided to go for and got cast. I didn't know much about the film at the time which turned out to be Baz Luhrmann's *Moulin Rouge*. I got the job, packed my bags and moved to Sydney. It was through that job that I got an agent and I started to work for everyone big in the Australian dance industry, including Jason Coleman and Kelley Abbey who I also

worked on *Happy Feet* 1 and 2 with.

Another highlight for me was being cast in *Singin' In The Rain*, the musical. At first I was the understudy for Sheree de Costa, and then I ended up taking over the role for the Australian and Asia tours.

WHAT QUALITIES DO YOU POSSESS THAT ALLOWED YOU TO HAVE SUCH A PROLIFIC CAREER AS A PERFORMER?

It is definitely work ethic and how you show up. I was always reliable and versatile so those choreographers knew that they could hire me and I would be able to do whatever they would ask me to do. Professionalism accounts for just as much as talent as far as I am concerned.

Now I am always talking about etiquette in class and how my dancers need to show up in the room. Work ethic is everything and what I like to teach children is that they are capable of a lot more than they think. When they think that they are sick, they think that they are tired, they need to push through those boundaries to really excel. You have to fight for it. I always ask them, "If you wanted me to write a recommendation for you, what would you want me to say about you?" Because recommendations and referrals matter. I try to teach them that they can be the best person they can be and work ethic, drive, dedication, all matters!

WHAT IS YOUR 'WHY'?

Back in my day we did not have Instagram, we did not have social media, we did not really know what was going on in the industry. I just had this drive to be the best dancer. I wanted to work with the best and work for the best. I was able to do that and then I got to a point later on in my career where I felt like I had so much to teach. I know the industry and I know what it takes to make it and what qualities you need, and I wanted to come back home to share that.

It is cliché and it is corny but I really did think if I could get one child to be able to live their dream like I did, then I will be happy. Because it is such a wonderful life. I honestly have had the best life, I had the best career, I met all of my best friends through dance and to be able to do what you love for a living is something that not a lot of people get to do. If I can help other children do that then that is everything.

Of course, studios evolve and there are children that do not want to do that, so my why now goes back to work ethic, and instilling good values in children so that it does not matter what they do in life, they will succeed. They will be able to take those lessons into whatever career they want to do.

WHO ARE YOUR BIGGEST ROLE MODELS, AND WHY?

Kelley Abbey was a huge inspiration now as well as when I was younger. She is so inspirational and you always learn from her, even as a professional dancer. Even in what she is doing today, Kelley is continually growing and evolving as an artist and that is really inspirational.

The other huge career and personal inspiration to me are actually two of my closest friends, Ashley and Antony – AKA The Squared Division. They are an inspiration for my age and I have seen them go from working dancers and artists and performers to grow to where they are now. They are huge creative directors in the USA and are just so successful. To watch them grow that business, I have so much respect and they inspire me so much. Their dedication to quality and staying true to themselves is a huge lesson that being confident and staying true to yourself works.

WHAT ARE SOME OF THE BIGGEST ADJUSTMENTS YOU HAVE MADE TO MEET CHANGES IN THE INDUSTRY OVER THE LAST TEN YEARS?

I keep hearing that there is not as much work now for dancers compared to back when I was dancing. We were constantly working because there was more TV and variety programs, so now there is potentially less work but a lot more dancers. There are a lot of pre-professional courses running at the moment so that training is a lot more accessible and the world has opened up more. We did not have a lot of dancers that dreamed of going to L.A. and dancing with artists back in my day, so now we work with our dancers to educate them and provide those larger opportunities to meet demand.

When it comes to social media, there is a lot that gets posted on Facebook and Instagram that is not actually a true reflection of what is happening in the industry. Instead, I see that we go through a lot more fads. We went through the stage where everyone wanted to put their leg up behind their head and they were posting that. Then it was a surge of hip-hop and there is a lot of jazz at the moment, and then lyrical became really popular. I have found that training children and reinforcing that they still have to do their ballet, musical theater to have any hope of a career as a performer. We teach them that dancing is not just about what happens in these videos.

WHAT DO YOU INCLUDE IN YOUR PROGRAMS FOR PRE-PROFESSIONAL DANCERS TO PREPARE THEM FOR A CAREER IN THE INDUSTRY?

Firstly, I make sure that I get teachers and trainers who have had extensive experience in the industry. There's a lot of great young choreographers out there that are teaching and that is awesome. There is a lot of value in those classes, but for me it is making sure I bring in experts and people that have been around for a long time, and making sure they learn from them as well. There is always the favorite young 'star' with great choreography that children want to get in, but I know that there is such a different value that comes from experienced teachers.

I really make sure that not only are they getting trained in all genres equally, but they are also being given the right business skills as well. It is about preparing them in a really well-rounded way.

Not all children love tap, not all children love ballet, not all children love joining musical theater, not all children want to learn how to sing – but they are going to. They have to. I was somebody, for instance, that wasn't a skilled singer, but my teacher made me choose singing lessons. I always had my private singing lessons and then years later, one of my career highlights was a musical theater show.

WHAT ARE SOME OF THE BIG BUSINESS MILESTONES THAT HIGHLIGHT YOUR TRANSITION TO BECOMING THE 'GO-TO' STUDIO?

I grew out of my first studio sooner than I thought, which was a big milestone. Within two years I started to look for a new space, and now I've got a space that is three times the size with five studios.

Launching our full-time pre-professional program was always my goal. When I got to do that – which included training up my students so they could feed that full-time course – that was a great moment.

I have just opened the agency too, which was all in my five year plan. There was a movie recently that filmed on the Gold Coast and they needed a group of dancers, and I remember thinking at the time, *I need to have an agency so I can take care of them.*

I always had the agency in sight, but it really pushed me to go. There is a big corporate scene up here too with event companies, so quite a lot of opportunities are starting to happen around town.

WHAT IS YOUR FAVORITE PIECE OF BUSINESS ADVICE?

My favorite one is, 'You've got to work ON your business, not IN it.'

That was what I planned straight off, because I was really working in my business and that push to hire the right staff to do those jobs was a big deal for me. I am still constantly trying to get out of my business too, and I am certainly not perfect at that, but I always have it in the back of my head. Especially as you grow, and keep growing, there is always that need to add somebody to delegate to.

I used to be scared of losing control. I wanted to have control over everything, but the realization that you just can't.

My first year, I was teaching 25 hours a week. I was doing all the inquiries, all of the emailing, everything possible. All of the concerts, pretty much doing everything and I had my mom doing my invoices and accounts and costumes. I remember getting to the end of that first year and thinking, *I don't know if I can keep doing this. I don't know how I am going to survive year after year, something has to change.*

HOW WOULD YOU DESCRIBE YOUR TRANSITION FROM THAT FIRST-YEAR STUDIO OWNER WHO DID EVERYTHING, TO THE LEADER YOU ARE TODAY?

I would have to say that my leadership is something that I am working on. To actually transition into that leadership role is a process. I am really lucky, my staff are so amazing and I feel like I have struck gold with my admin staff and my front desk. I am still so lucky to have my mom working in that business as well, having that trust with my team. I am definitely becoming more confident as a leader. I am sure of what I want and of the vision I have for the studio.

At first, I really struggled to communicate if I was not happy with something, and I am getting better at that.

I have so much admiration for how committed my next featured Dance Studio Owner is to her personal growth as the CEO of her studio as well as her commitment to the arts in her local area. Since I first met her two years ago, Lindsay has had an unwavering focus on building a strong performing arts culture in her local area and generously shares this passion with our Inner Circle members daily.

Lindsay Prather is the CEO of Jitterbug Performing Arts in Georgia, USA.

What began as a travelling program in various schools quickly grew into the busy studio that Jitterbug Performing Arts is today. Since 2011, Jitterbug programming has allowed students to express their creative side, build confidence, and develop their natural talents. While building her business, she also married her best friend with whom she had two beautiful children, who challenge and inspire her daily.

In 2018, she set out on a second venture with her husband to create steamBug, a makerspace for children, with the same mission of building confidence in the next generation; using science, technology, engineering, art and math to empower children to think with both sides of the brain, fusing logic with creativity.

To this day her favorite part of this work is seeing parents' eyes fill with tears when their child overcomes fear, grows beyond what they think is possible, or nails something they've been practicing for weeks. Being part of empowering the next generation of creatives is more fulfilling than she ever dreamed.

Check out Lindsay's latest studio news at jitterbugperformingarts. com

Chapter Six

BEING FEARLESS WITH YOUR STUDIO VISION: LINDSAY PRATHER

Jitterbug Performing Arts

50 YEARS FROM NOW, WHAT WOULD YOU LIKE YOUR LEGACY TO BE AS THE CEO OF JITTERBUG PERFORMING ARTS?

The biggest thing for me is just being able to empower the next generation of children to be their best selves and have the confidence to go and do whatever they wanted to do, whether it was in performing arts or not. But also really to nurture and empower them to be present in the world. Technology has become everything to children. Every child is addicted to it in some way or another. I, at that time, was focusing on a lot of babysitting and nannying and there were children who would go on playdates and they would just sit together on their tablets and play games the whole time. It was really a big moment for me where I just recognized how important it was to be able to keep that creative part of their brain going and the connection between children and their parents.

I saw performing arts as a way to nurture that, and to build that, and to grow that outside of the technology world.

I really had just always had a drive to do things for myself. If there is somebody doing something, I want to find a better way to do it. I also wanted a very specific lifestyle when I went into having a family. This was my way to achieve that. So, I knew with the lifestyle that I wanted in the performing arts I was going to have to do something different to be able to raise my children. Running the studio has been a way for me to:

a) Do what I love. That's something else I want – to show my children and my dancers that whatever it is that you want to do, find what you love to do and then make that your job.

b) Continue pursuing my love for performing and musical theater in a sustainable way, and

c) I really love figuring things out for my own and finding good ways to do things and running things the way I really felt that they needed to run. And I combined that all into building the studio of my dreams.

WHO INSPIRES YOU TO CONSISTENTLY LIFT YOUR GAME IN BUSINESS?

I don't necessarily know that I have one main role model or inspiration. I really think that children are the biggest inspiration. Being able to see what hole can we fill for them and for their development.

I really feel like that has been my biggest career inspiration. The different students that we have and what they are dealing with in their lives, whether it's personal, or performing arts-wise, or family-wise. What can we fill, what can we get them that's going to fill them up and push them to be better people in the world?

There was one studio that I worked for and the owner just was never there. Everything was just left to us, and there were no systems. It was "Figure it out!". It wasn't fair on the staff, but ended up great for me, because I did figure it out and could draw on that experience when the time came for me to open my own studio.

I previously worked for a non-profit which really left a bad taste in my mouth because this particular one was not about the children. It made all this money and had all of these donations coming in and there was such a tiny amount of that went to do any good. I hated that, and I hated that I was the one that was doing it. I had no control over the money. I did what I was told. I was scheduled where I was scheduled. I knew what I was getting paid to do these workshops for the underprivileged, but I also knew how much money and fame was being given to this organization and it just rubbed me the wrong way.

I have seen a lot of gaps as well when it comes to customer experience. So often there is a lot of attention that was given to the 'gold star' students and nothing put in place for the rest of the studio. It can be so hard when there are no standards for anything. When there are so many questions and not having the answers to things as an employee it made things really hard.

That was something that was super important going forward for me, to make sure whoever is answering questions has the information they need.

I've worked in studios where nothing was ever done the way that it needed to be done. There was no praise, there was no joy. It was all about money. It wasn't about the positive experience, it was "Well are they going to do two classes? Well are they going to do six classes?" Or "Have they paid yet?" So, everything was all about the money. It was not about the child's experience, it was not about the parent's experience, and it was not about the staff's experience.

I definitely use those experiences as inspiration for the atmosphere that I want to have because for me, it's really important to not do that.

WHAT QUALITIES MAKE YOU A GREAT BOSS TO WORK UNDER?

I definitely think I am fearless. I just know what is meant to be and have confidence that we're going to figure it out. Sometimes that can be a little bit more challenging than I anticipate, but it needs to happen.

I'm probably a little bit too empathetic. I think it is very good to have empathy with your staff and with your families, but sometimes there's only so much you can do. Sometimes I have a hard time separating myself with that.

We've spent a lot of time nurturing our staff in the last year. That is something that I am very proud of that we come from a very nurturing, growth, empowering point of view and having my office separate was a game changer for that. Because I was able to process things and think about how I wanted to talk to them about it, before the moment happened. If somebody needs to come tell me about a mistake that was made or something that's not going well, we have a separate space to do that that's not in the middle of everything happening.

Moving into my own space has really been instrumental in my

reactions and the way that I act as a CEO. It's removed me from that day-to-day moment. It's been good for them and it's been good for me because it's definitely made me a better leader and more encouraging as the CEO.

WHAT IS YOUR JITTERBUG 'SPECIAL SAUCE' THAT MAKES YOUR PRESCHOOL CLASSES SO SUCCESSFUL?

The parents, especially that age group, are just as much a focus as the child. The classes are 45 minutes and we do not have parents in our classes at that age group. But seeing them and interacting with them afterwards and having that energy works wonders. We are really particular about our atmosphere and our energy from our teachers and our admin staff and have a very specific type of person who connects with the child and the parents.

It's about when they come out of class, how they can celebrate their wins and just really keeping them updated throughout the semester. At that age to both the child and the parent, everything is new and everything is exciting.

The parents are so in tune and they just want to soak up every little tidbit. Giving them those extra details about their child in class – whether it's something funny they said or did – is crucial. It really makes them feel heard and like we know their child. That is such a huge part of our program is making sure that the parents feel valued for that age group as well as the child. We keep our class sizes relatively small and having those moments with each child are a key part of them

trusting you and them building their confidence.

Our studio is confidence first and technique second. Having that confidence is what's going to make the child want to come back, too. When the parent is happy and hearing about their child, and the child is also falling in love with that and wanting to come back and enjoy their experience, I feel like that is the whole picture.

WHAT WOULD BE YOUR TOP THREE PIECES OF ADVICE FOR ANY STUDIO OWNERS WHO MAY BE DOUBTING THEMSELVES IN THEIR EARLY DAYS?

The biggest one would be just believe in yourself. I had a really significant turning point last year when I joined the Dance Studio Owners Inner Circle and really felt empowered to not care what anybody says.

I've spent my whole life just trying to make other people happy. I'm definitely a people pleaser and I try to do everything in my power to make sure that everybody's happy all the time. And that is not realistic. Especially as the studio grows, and our staff grows, and our students grow, it is impossible. Every day there is somebody that is unhappy about something. It took me a long time to get over that. And if I could have done something differently earlier on, it would be to let the small things go and to really make sure that I'm looking at the full picture and not the individual moment.

Secondly, being young it was really hard to have that distinction between co-workers, friends, and bosses. It was a really tricky combination and I wish that I could have told myself to not be anybody's friend. There was a point in time where it was incredibly lonely. But I decided that I had to make that break and I couldn't be anybody's friend. Because you just can't manage them when you're there, trying to be their friend and go out at night for a drink. It was too messy. You can still empower them, and support them, and love them without that friendship element.

Finally, always follow your gut. If something feels right, then it's going to fall into place and you'll figure out how to get there. That is really how we've grown so much and I wouldn't want to change that. Put as much focus and energy as you can into your plan A and not running yourself into the ground. Because that's what you'd have to do if you're thinking about plans A, B, C, and D.

Having those boundaries in place is really important. That's something else that has been a big change for me in the last year, being able to set those family and personal boundaries before the work boundaries. There's been many a time when I have run myself into the ground and it's taken a long time to recover from that. If you focus on plan A and don't worry about the rest, then you don't spend as much energy and it's more sustainable.

DANCE STUDIO SECRETS BONUS –
IF YOU'D LIKE TO EXPERIENCE STUDIO GROWTH AND FREEDOM LIKE LINDSAY, MAKE SURE TO CHECK OUT OUR FREE STUDIO GROWTH VIDEO TRAINING AT
DSOA.COM/BONUS-GROWTH

In this chapter you'll meet one of the first Dance Studio Owners I ever worked with, and continue to coach to this day. Rebecca's superpower – and what I believe the secret of her success – is the clarity she has for her studio's path. She's never been afraid of what other people are saying or doing, and is 100% focused and committed on where she wants to take her students while blocking out the noise and distractions around her.

Rebecca Liu-Brennan is the CEO of Performance Art Western Sydney (PAWS) in New South Wales, Australia.

Rebecca realized her dream of owning her own dance school and helping other aspiring dancers and performers to achieve their own goals when she established Performance Art Western Sydney (PAWS) in 2005.

She studied at the Central Coast College of Dance and Tanya Pearson Classical Coaching Academy before dancing professionally in Japan with the Ikagami Ballet Company. She has also performed with the Garry Spellman Show, Australian Elvis Festival, Breen Machine and in the short film *Duk-duk*.

Rebecca is a sought-after teacher and choreographer who has taught for Sydney Dance Company Studios, Alegeria, JTV Dance and Entertainment, Bradford Dance Academy, Dance Junction, Dancentral, Dance Tech 2000, Mango Dance Studios and Helen Haskis Studio of Dance.

Rebecca is the proud mom to BeBe and Phoenix, and loves nothing more than relaxing with a glass of wine and a great biography.

Check out Bec's latest studio news at pawstudios.com

Chapter Seven

FROM SURVIVING TO THRIVING IN BUSINESS AND LIFE: REBECCA LIU-BRENNAN

PAWS

WHAT WAS THE BIGGEST SURPRISE DURING YOUR FIRST YEAR OF RUNNING THE DANCE STUDIO?

Definitely how many costs were involved with running a business. I say this to my teachers all the time as well and my student teachers if they have aspirations to run their own business or work as a contractor – they just don't realize how much a business actually costs to run and neither did I because I certainly was not a business person. Wages, electricity, supplies, building costs, marketing, branding etc.

When you don't own a business you don't realize the extra costs there are on top of everything, and that they just keep accumulating. A lot of dance studios think that the answer to their financial problems is to just get more students, but it doesn't work like that. More students simply means more overheads, so getting smart around finance is absolutely crucial.

WHAT IS SOMETHING THAT YOU HAVE FAILED AT, AND WHAT LESSONS DID YOU TAKE AWAY?

Unfortunately, I have to say my marriage. I didn't think my marriage was going to go so badly, and my ex-husband was my business partner which made things incredibly difficult when going through our separation and divorce five years ago. It was so hard to understand going from the happiness that we had just disappear into a downward spiral.

I literally left him with a suitcase and a baby, and had to erase that from my whole life while trying to work out how to pay $102,000 to get custody of my child and keep the business. I finished paying that debt off last year, which was a huge moment for me.

The biggest lesson I took away from those hard years and that failure was the importance of my support network. Having support from my best friends, my mentor and my team held me up, and helped me focus on what I needed to do. If I didn't have those support systems I would never have continued.

I also learned about the importance of having solid business systems in place. I would never have pushed through to where I did and I wouldn't have been able to afford the time and financial investment in legal costs just to get through what I had to to survive. If those business systems weren't in place to keep the business running without me there, I wouldn't be here today with a studio at all, let alone a thriving one.

WHAT IS THE PROJECT THAT YOU ARE PASSIONATE ABOUT RIGHT NOW AND WHY DOES IT MEAN SO MUCH TO YOU?

One big project I am so excited about is a new business venture within the studio, called Teacher Tribe, which is a teacher training program where I am working with other studios to train and upskill their staff.

We work on goal-setting with teachers as well as goal-setting strategies to use with students. We also work on having a 'theme' in the studio each quarter and each team member is responsible for an initiative that encapsulates that theme. For example, one theme might be 'Confidence'. One of my teachers came to us with an idea to write an individual card for every child in their class to say what they improved in. Another strategy might be receiving a star, or a grading when dancers achieve a new skill, so it's both showing progression and building confidence at the same time.

These may be strategies that come quite easily to the minds of studio owners, but the whole point is to stay quiet and allow your staff to think about it and come up with their own ideas. They are also so much more invested in the implementation of these ideas too.

We talk about how to make every child feel special within their own parameters, within their own abilities, and I do a walk-through with teachers, and role-play the customer journey to see what happens when each new student arrives at the studio to try a class.

For example, we might ask two teachers to stand in the lobby and pretend to be talking and ignore the new student. Then we will yell "PAUSE" and have another team member jump in and demonstrate what it would look like to actually approach that student. It sounds simple, but acting these roles out sticks in their memory ten times more than if I just told them to do it.

I like to also train teachers for the non-dance elements within a dance class. What happens if that student screams throughout the whole lesson? What happens to that student if they don't want to join in at first? We workshop techniques on how to help those children. Teachers in the training love it, because they get an opportunity to give feedback on ideas on how to talk to parents which is often the hardest thing that teachers have to do. They are so used to technology, they aren't equipped to deal with conflict.

One of the most talked-about sessions we run is on strategies for cleaning choreography for younger dancers by using games like musical statues.

YOU HAVE A HOLISTIC APPROACH TO YOUR DANCERS IN TERMS OF THEIR OVERALL WELL-BEING BOTH INSIDE AND OUTSIDE THE DANCE CLASS. WHAT PROMPTED THIS FOCUS, AND WHAT DO YOU DO IN CLASS TO NURTURE THIS?

It all started because I was having difficulties with my own child getting her to sleep at night, as well as getting her off screens. I was looking for ways to get her motivated to set goals, and it dawned on me that if I am having this problem other people must be having this problem.

We run a two-day workshop called 'Soul Tribe' where we bring in professionals to talk to our dancers about nutrition, goal setting and mindfulness. We do a vision board workshop with them, and have professional athletes come to talk to them about resilience. We also run a workshop for parents so that they can actually find out and get some experience with what these children have been working on. We give the parents recipes and teach meditation techniques for their dancers to settle down at night for a decent sleep.

WHAT HAS MADE YOU SO SUCCESSFUL AS A STUDIO OWNER IN A NICHE WHEN MANY OTHERS HAVE FAILED?

Developing children so that they are able to fit into the entertainment business has been a big thing, so making sure children are at a level that a corporate agent will take on, is really important.

When it comes to running professional events and entertainment opportunities, we worked hard to find the formula that entertains children and makes them excited to watch the show. We have interactive dances the audience absolutely loves, because they can join in. We use choreography that our dancers already know, and keep it simple with costuming and backdrops that can be used for a variety of themes.

Another big game changer for our paid shows is hiring an amazing narrator so that even if the dancing is not so great that day, the narrator can fill those gaps.

WHAT ARE THE TOP THREE QUALITIES YOU THINK ARE THE MOST IMPORTANT WHEN YOU ARE HIRING A NEW TEACHER?

The most important quality of a dance teacher for younger dancers is having a sense of humor – being able to make the children laugh and enjoy their classes. That is absolutely the most important thing as those children will be coming back for more, and teachers don't realize that.

The next important thing is teaching children to reflect on themselves, because if you tell them why they have to do it and how it actually makes them improve, then they are going to care a bit more about it. I don't think teachers think about that side of things enough.

The third quality would be allowing children to be at their own level, not expecting everyone to be the top dancer of the group. Letting them be okay with the fact that they are at their own level and helping them to understand those amazing things. That is the key to keeping every child in the class, because we are all going to have amazing children on the frontline but what's more important is making those back line children feel special.

IF I WAS A STARTUP STUDIO OWNER HAVING LUNCH WITH YOU, WHAT QUESTIONS SHOULD I BE ASKING YOU TO GET THE MOST OUT OF OUR TIME TOGETHER?

How do I structure my business so that I am not constantly working 24 hours a day, seven days a week? Because when you first start a business and you don't know anything about business, then you are just constantly running and you never actually have anything in place to alleviate that.

For example, we have our whole year planned out in Asana software, so every day everyone will just see exactly what they are doing, what's happening next, and who's the project manager.

I would also ask, 'How do you manage your staff?'. A lot of studio owners don't even want to talk to their staff, don't want to tell their staff they are doing things wrong. You can't run a successful business like that.

I'd finally ask about managing family/work balance. I make a promise to myself that at seven o'clock, I go off my phone. My phone goes away and I'm in the moment with my children. In the mornings I try not to get on my phone until they are dropped to daycare, just so that I have that consistent quality time.

I am so thrilled to introduce you to our next featured Dance Studio CEO, Courtney Sproule. Courtney comes from a corporate background and from the moment I met her I knew she had great business acumen. She runs an extraordinary business and  **has built a strong culture with her team members. Courtney has so much gold to share when it comes to running a successful dance studio where her team members love coming to work every day.**

Courtney Sproule is the CEO of Snap Dance Studios in Alberta, Canada.

At the age of three, Courtney couldn't help but follow in the footsteps of her siblings and twinkle her toes in dance class. She formally trained in Calgary at Premiere Dance Academy, Danscott Studio, and Expressions the Dance Gallery, as well as at the EDGE in Los Angeles, Broadway Dance Centre in New York and Pineapple Studios in London.

Courtney has performed throughout Australia, New Zealand, England, France and the United States at venues such as EuroDisney, Walt Disney World and Universal Studios. Locally, she has performed with En Corps Dance Collective, a contemporary dance company in Calgary, and played the role of Diana Morales in the musical *A Chorus Line*. In 2006, she was lucky enough to be selected as an ambassador for Lululemon Athletica.

Courtney has a Communications Degree and has held numerous marketing and communication positions. She has also dabbled in the art of recruiting, but now focuses her efforts full time on Snap.

Check out Courtney's latest studio news at snapdancestudios. com

Chapter Eight

CREATING A CULTURE OF EMPOWERMENT: COURTNEY SPROULE

Snap Dance Studios

WHEN DID YOU FIRST KNOW THAT YOU WANTED TO OPEN A DANCE STUDIO?

I started dancing at a young age, and my parents always said, "We invested in your dance, so that's what you should use to get your post-secondary." I taught dance all the way through my degree in communications, and the stars just aligned and things happened for me to own my school.

The last year of my degree is when I opened the studio in a partnership, but I also had this dream of wanting to work downtown. Or so I thought. I remember getting downtown my first day in a work co-op and realizing... this is just boring! I worked for about eight years downtown and I'm lucky I was young because it was just so hard splitting my time between a business and a job.

I learned a lot of things from my day job about business, communications, recruiting, and how to work with teams. I got a lot of that experience, thankfully, but then finally in 2010 I just knew it was time for a drastic change. In the last couple of years of splitting the job and the business, I was exhausted, and I constantly felt like I was always being pulled in two directions.

And that's when it happened. I bought another studio, and fast-forward to today where now it's been ten years.

WHAT ARE SOME OF THE BIGGEST LESSONS YOU LEARNED IN TAKING OVER AN EXISTING STUDIO?

Well, I've been through it all! I bought out a business partner, and then ran it on my own before adding on an existing studio. When it comes to buying an established studio, you just have to be open. I was really open to the other owner's advice. She had a really strong preschool program and I was really open to listening to her and what she had to say about her program and learning from that.

I wanted those clients to come on board and felt that even though they had chosen that other studio, I wanted them to see the value in us while being open to hearing their feedback, concerns and advice. We did workshop classes with them, and I went to their recital to do a speech on stage to build that connection and add value.

You just have to take it step by step, read the right signs for you and your community, and not freak out about it. There are so many times in a business where things are just crazy, and you have to slow down and see your way through it and assess the next right step.

WHAT IS YOUR 'WHY'?

For me, dance changed my life. And so now it is about changing the lives of children for the better, in a positive way through dance. It's interesting because obviously as we grow our businesses, the goal is to get bigger and get more income through the door. But I don't have a great relationship with money, and I had this big 'A-ha!' moment two years ago when I finally realized it isn't about the money.

It is about the more children you have in the studio and the more things they do, the more opportunity we have to change their lives. And literally that's what it's about for us now.

I came from a family of three and we couldn't afford to do everything. I couldn't be in the production or have a solo that year because my siblings had to dance too, but those were great lessons because I wanted it so bad and it was so good for me to not get everything. I learned that there's just so many ways it changed my life for the better, and

I got to travel all over the world with dance and build extraordinary friendships.

That's why I do it.

And now that's so much easier. I have this conversation every year with my staff at our kickoff meeting where I share my why and making them see that it actually isn't about the dollars – it's actually about changing the lives of these children.

These children are the future city planners, our future nurses, our future doctors. We are investing in them and it really transcends into so many different areas.

WHO ARE YOUR ROLE MODELS, AND WHY?

Firstly, it would have to be my parents. They were both working; my mom was a school teacher; my dad was a principal. And now you realize the struggle is really being a parent! Working, and running a business is a whole different thing, but they gave me unconditional love and they worked so hard to allow me to dance.

I've also had some connections through the Dance Studio Owners Inner Circle with other studio owners – finally people who get you! These women have become like sisters to me, and it's such an amazing relationship to have people that you can call.

I used to feel so alone at night when something's going down at the dance studio because you get emotionally invested, but now having people to call has made such a difference.

My last huge source of inspiration are some of the phenomenal leaders in the emotional intelligence space. Oprah, Brene Brown, Clint Salter to name just a few because you understand that it isn't about just the business. It's about your overall happiness, your staff's overall happiness, and your client's happiness.

WHAT ARE YOUR TOP THREE TIPS FOR STUDIO OWNERS WHO MAY BE STRUGGLING WITH WORK/LIFE BALANCE?

It's all still a work in progress but shutting off when you come home or when it's not work time anymore is a big priority for me. And setting those boundaries around what hours I work or what projects I work on.

It's a continual process of me trying to figure out roles in my organization and making sure that expectations are really clear so my team can do an amazing job without me jumping in all the time. It's also about setting up training and systems to get your business to support that too.

WHAT MAKES YOUR STUDIO UNIQUE?

Culturally you can always go through ups and downs in your studio, but I am really focused in on our studio culture and the big things that are important to me.

I always say to people, "We focus on your child as a dancer and as a human." It's about the whole person – we aren't just training a dancer. The dancer and the human part is important and we are always really trying to be a positive and inclusive environment for everybody. We don't just focus on training and technique... it's a balance between the two while also being about the community.

We have exceptional customer service and I always want people to be surprised by the level of care and consideration.

HAVE YOU HAD ANY 'A-HA' MOMENTS THAT HAVE SHAPED YOUR BUSINESS?

So many! A big one was when I realized that it's not about the money anymore, it's about changing children's lives. Another moment would be when I decided that culturally I really want to be a strong studio and knew deep down that I wanted to be more than just about dancing and technique. I want it to be about the team, not about one person on that team.

Another huge moment was signing on to the Dance Studio Owners Inner Circle. To be honest, it was really scary because I had never done anything that big.

I now know that it's okay to say no and that you can't please everyone, which is hard for me because I *want* to please everyone. And I *want* to be everything. While I know that less is more, I'm really trying to work on this one slowly because I *want* to do everything.

It has been so crucial for me to find my tribe and accept that people who you don't align with will find their tribe, and that it's okay to come to peace with that. Most of the time people who leave for another studio or tribe end up in a better place that works for them while you just do what's right for you.

Now I'm in such a better place when I see former students. I used to be constantly asking myself, "What did I do wrong?" Now, I maybe did do some things wrong but, in the moment, I made the best decision I could. They seem so happy, and I wish them happiness knowing that all our stars can shine bright whether we're together in a dance studio or if people decide to go elsewhere.

HOW WOULD YOU DESCRIBE YOURSELF AS THE CEO OF YOUR STUDIO?

My motto is: Forever Learning.

It is hard for me to step into the CEO role because I do want to help and be involved in everything. I'm trying to stand strong in my position, and I'm feeling a big shift even this year to lead more. I kept jumping down to help with things and now I'm trying to stay out and let my team of very smart, capable women do their thing so I can focus on my job and do it well.

I don't necessarily think it is a bad quality – we were all teachers, we all were the administrator, we've all run credit card payments. I've done every single job in that studio. Sometimes you may be afraid to let go, or it may be your ego thinking, *I just need to teach them the right way.*

The best thing is that we want to help, we want to be a team member, we want to show you that you can roll up your sleeves and help. And there are for sure moments for that, but I had done it a lot. I'm having to shift my thinking and even shift my team's thinking to understand that I'm better served here, and you're better served there.

My husband is a pilot and he doesn't go back to help with food service or safety instructions. He flies the plane. If there's a problem with an unruly passenger, they'll keep him updated. That is their job. There's a whole bunch of competent staff back there to deal with it because he's got to fly the plane, right?

So, I'm learning to fly the plane.

WHAT ARE THE BIGGEST LESSONS THAT YOU HAVE LEARNED IN THE NON-DANCE WORLD THAT HAVE REALLY TRANSLATED OVER TO HOW YOU RUN YOUR STUDIO NOW?

I was talking to another studio owner that had a communications background, and just how important that is. Most of our dance parents are women and they like knowing what's going on. They may not read the newsletter. So, you text them, you have it on Facebook, you put up posters. You really need to be there for the crazy-busy working mom.

Knowing you have so many audiences to communicate to is relationship building. I would always have this conversation with my friends. One was an engineer, one was a trailer salesman, and one was an accountant. We asked the question: what part of your job is training that you learned in school, and what part of your job is just relationship building? And everyone said more than 50% is relationships and just being able to understand social situations and navigate things.

Even the engineer. She drills million-dollar wells for oil and gas, and she has to work with rig people and develop a relationship with them because they may be annoyed that there's a woman calling the shots. To get the job done efficiently and safely, communication is the key for her to break down those barriers.

ONCE YOU ENROLL A NEW STUDENT HOW DO YOU KEEP THEM?

It's not about just teaching dance anymore – it's about this event and that experience.

We have an automated onboarding process that is systemized with the Inner Circle 11-step enrollment process. A big thing for us is events. Competitions, showcases, community performances and social events.

We have a competition launch party the night before we have a competition. The children get in small groups, they each make up a cheer then we will vote on the best cheer, then we sit down and talk about, "What happens if someone says something really rude at competition? How do you handle that?" And "If we do really well at competition or we don't do well, what's our reaction? Let's think about that. Do you squeal and scream if you win something? You have to think about other people standing on the stage that didn't win, right? But then also on the other hand, when you don't get what you want, should you be a blubbering mess? It's okay to have those emotions, but let's also be respectful and think about others, let's be empathetic of others."

It's coaching them as children and it's also a human piece at the same time.

WHAT DO YOU THINK IS THE BIGGEST CHALLENGE WHEN IT COMES TO RUNNING A THRIVING DANCE STUDIO?

What I'm learning is that the biggest challenge is 'time'. To get done what you need to do and what you want to do. We can exhaust ourselves as studio owners, and teachers, and everyone in this industry. I don't really think people understand when they bring their child to dance and even when their child dances a zillion hours, how much work goes into that.

Time is the biggest challenge, and figuring out your time, and whether you have a small studio or a big studio, and how to use your time well and use your time for you, both personally, but also for the values that you want and what you want to get out of life.

People are what make your business go around. Your clients, your staff, your teachers, and it all comes down to values. It all comes down to the values, and do you share those values? Some of the big struggles I've had with teachers or clients comes down to a value clash. I used to get all flustered about it, now I understand that it's okay to not be perfect. I always wanted to please everyone.

You also must find the right professional development and coaching for you. I was the hamster on the wheel. I was running. And you have to get off the wheel, you have to get off the wheel! You have to look around, and you need to figure out, *Do I still need to do this? What needs to change?*

I had to really figure out how to create time and space for the things I wanted in my life. I do have enough time, and I must make a change if I want to see results and I want to see a shift.

Over the coming pages of this book you are going to meet a Dance Studio CEO with such a bright spirit that it will jump off the pages. Whether it's on a coaching call or at an in-person Inner Circle retreat, Angela always lights up a room. She is also extremely invested in ensuring that her students are becoming better humans every time they enter her studio.

Angela Mannella-Hoffman is the Owner and Artistic Director of Moore Than Dance in Fridley, Minnesota USA. Known for her creativity and passion, Angela has developed original programming for her studio including 'Movin' with the Moose!' preschool musical theater and dance classes and 'Special Stars' classes for those with special needs.

Angela started acting professionally at the age of eight. Her theater credits include: The Guthrie Theater, The Children's Theater Company, Shakespeare and Company, MN, Minnesota Shakespeare Project, Hennepin Stages, and many other local and regional theaters.

She has acted in over 300 commercials and industrials. Angela is an active voice-over actress, lending her voice to companies such as 3M, Cargill, and Target.

Dance credits include: Loyce Houlton's Nutcracker Fantasy, Super Bowl XXVI, Paul McCartney's Back in the US tour, and many industrials and plays where she was the dance captain.

Angela lives in Minnesota with her husband and son. She loves spending time with her eight brothers and sisters, friends and extended family.

Check out Angela's latest studio news at moorethandance.com

Chapter Nine

IT'S ABOUT MORE THAN DANCING: ANGELA MANNELLA-HOFFMAN

Moore Than Dance LLC

TELL US ABOUT BACKGROUND IN DANCE AND PERFORMING ARTS, AND HOW THAT EVOLVED IN TO YOU OPENING YOUR STUDIO?

Well, I started acting professionally when I was eight doing a lot of theater and commercials and I went on tour with different professional shows and performances. While I always was a great dancer, I never quite fit the body type that was needed.

And I wasn't a great singer.

So I continued professionally through adulthood acting, dancing and doing a little bit of singing before I started teaching for other studios. That's when I noticed – quite devastatingly – that a lot of my gorgeous students were really body conscious... which started to really bother me.

I kept thinking about what I would do differently if I had my own space and my own studio.

Fast forward a few months and one day my husband was driving by and saw that there was a dance studio building for sale, and something just clicked. We looked into it and that's where we started.

We started back then with the one studio and now we have three thriving studios. I realize now that my whole life I've been preparing for this, but I never knew I was.

WHAT DID YOU WANT TO DO DIFFERENTLY FROM OTHER STUDIOS YOU HAD SEEN OR WORKED AT THAT YOU KNEW FROM DAY ONE WAS REALLY GOING TO SET YOU APART?

One of the first things I wanted to do was to incorporate singing, dancing and acting so all of our students really can be triple threats. We also started to bring in guest teachers, experts, and leaders who talk to them about the profession and how they can really make the most out of every minute in the studio.

The main reason I wanted to do this was because of my own experiences having been in both a studio and a ballet company when I was growing up, I always had a foot in both of those doors and could take away lessons from both.

Even more important to me though was to make it a priority at our studio to let the children really feel and understand that they are a gift, and that it doesn't matter what their body type is.

I want them to know that anybody can dance, and anybody can sing. While our culture started with a focus on body-image and confidence, it has also evolved to a point where we now teach a lot of students with special needs who wouldn't fit a typical type of dance class or studio.

We also do a full-length musical every other year where we bring in an orchestra, sets, and lights and go to a different theater and all of our students are included in that. It's a very inclusive place.

WHAT KINDS OF STRATEGIES DO YOU USE IN CLASS TO COMBAT THE NEGATIVE BODY-IMAGE THAT IS SUCH AN ISSUE FOR YOUNG DANCERS IN OUR INDUSTRY?

We do a lot of journaling in and out of the classroom. At the beginning of the season, I give each of my competition and teen dancers their own journal and I write little notes and affirmations in it scattered throughout the journal which they'll open up on different days.

I also share my experiences a lot, especially with my older dancers. I've talked with them about my memories of my ballet teacher pulling me in front of the whole class to demonstrate how fat I was and that I would never be a dancer. I tell them that they are a gift from God – that wherever they are at, that's who they are and it's nothing to feel ashamed about... or that it's something they have to change.

Another huge thing, especially for this age group, is that we don't allow phones in the classroom at all.

For my younger dancers, we find so many opportunities to use the power of language to reiterate what a gift they are. They may say, "My legs are tired; I can't keep dancing." This alone is such a great teaching opportunity to remind them how blessed they are to have legs that work! Even little exercises where we bend over and stretch and say, "Thank you, thighs, for keeping me up today." I try to incorporate silliness with it and other funny little things so it's not like beating them over the head with a lesson!

WHAT ARE SOME OF THE BIGGEST LESSONS FROM YOUR CAREER AS A PERFORMER THAT HAVE HELPED YOU IN RUNNING THE STUDIO SO SUCCESSFULLY?

The first one was how well I could survive on no money in the early days! I had to make sacrifices, obviously, but that really helped me those first couple of years because I knew that it wasn't the end of the world if my bank account wasn't quite where I wanted it to be and to stay patient and consistent.

Another thing I learned is how important it is to be a triple threat. If our students want to be professional performers, they need to know how to sing, act and perform. That was really valuable to me when opening the studio.

But the biggest lesson was just being grateful for every opportunity. I was always so grateful for any job and I'm still so grateful for any family that comes to our studio. It's a gift to me that these dance families are allowing me to teach and work with them, so I never take that for granted.

WHAT WERE THE THREE BIGGEST MILESTONES THAT DEFINED YOUR TRANSITION FROM TEACHER TO CEO?

The biggest one was joining the Dance Studio Owners Inner Circle, which really opened my eyes to everything. I remember the first Inner Circle retreat where we were talking about stepping out of teaching, and it just blew my mind. I remember you saying that, and I'd never thought of that before!

Another big one was getting my own office within the studio. I had always worked at the front desk when other people weren't, but when I finally got my own little office... that really made me feel more like the CEO.

The third milestone was hiring a great office manager. That took a lot off my plate and also gave me the confidence that it was done in a really professional way instead of me dropping the ball on things.

HOW WOULD YOUR TEAM DESCRIBE YOU AS A LEADER?

I think they would say I'm creative and passionate, not very detail-oriented and much more of a big picture kind of thinker. I also think they may say I'm larger than life sometimes!

Before I hired my office manager and admin team, I always knew that I wasn't very organized or detailed, but I realize now that your brain can only hold so much. It's helpful to know that that's not a weakness. It's just a different way of doing things and having the right team on board to carry any 'slack'.

I also think my team would say I'm consistent, and this is where I believe communication has been so important. We do a once a month zoom meeting with all the 12 teachers, and I do a weekly meeting with my office staff. Our office manager also does a weekly meeting with the other two front desk people, so we're consistent with checking in on everybody at least once a month.

ON THE TOPIC OF BIG-PICTURE THINKING, WHAT STRATEGIES DO YOU THINK HAVE HAD THE BIGGEST IMPACT ON THE GROWTH OF YOUR STUDIO?

One thing for me was setting up the Inner Circle re-enrollment process before the season ended.

I started doing it and that is a game changer because then you have engaged with those dancers and you can also predict your numbers for the next season. Now we do a re-enrollment packet for our students, and I have office hours where parents can meet with me for 15 minutes and go over what they want for their children.

Another strategy that has made a huge impact on our student retention and values-based culture has been our Thankful Tree. That is a huge feature in our studio every November that has really become locally famous around our studio and on social media.

I give each of my teachers a foam leaf or a foam pumpkin, and they write something that they are thankful for each and every one of our students. An example might be: "Jenny, I'm thankful that you smile every day in the beginning of class." And then they sign it and we stick it on to a huge paper tree that we put up in the lobby on November 1.

In the last week of November, right before Thanksgiving, they can take their leaf home. So, it's up for about a month and we do a lot of social media around it, get a lot of pictures, and it's really sweet and fun for children to find their leaf you can see them just beaming. It also makes the teachers feel great as well and has definitely impacted on our culture as well as staff retention.

WHAT ARE YOUR FAVORITE BUSINESS RESOURCES THAT YOU WOULD RECOMMEND, AND WHY?

Well, the first one for me is the Bible, just because I try to live by those philosophies in business and life. So when I am feeling guilty perhaps about making money or things like that, the Bible is my go-to.

Also, an absolute favorite of mine is the Daily Greatness business planner. It has different resources every week you think about and reflect on; it has questions for each day (for example, list my top three income producing activities). When you reflect back on your week, there are questions like, "How did I show up as CEO?" or "What three things do I need to eliminate to get more clarity?"

Another book from a long time ago that I often think about as it aligns with my business is *Jonathan Livingston Seagull*. There's a line in that book that says, "Jonathan Livingston Seagull, do you want to fly?" And he says, "Yes, I want to fly."

But it's not about flying, or excelling at all – it's about the things that he needs to leave in order to reach the higher level.

So that to me is such an inspirational thing and it reminds me of how you're going to have to move to different levels, let go of toxic people, let go of drama, and sometimes let go of people who have been outgrown by the studio.

WHAT ARE THE KEY INGREDIENTS TO YOUR PRESCHOOL CLASS 'SPECIAL SAUCE'?

What I love about the preschool age group is that they always look for a sense of magic.

I love seeing them just light up whenever we do a movement that has some imagination behind it. We do our Arabesques to 'Angel En-Fasse', where we reach up high into the clouds and do our arabesque and say, "Hello to 'Angel En-Fasse'" and they all just think that's the MOST fun. I use the correct terminology but create something special and magical around it.

The biggest thing for preschoolers is that you just really have to see them as little people. They are these little tiny seeds that you have to water and take care of.

Whenever students come in to the studio, I always bend down to the level of the littlest child and talk to them, and that always makes a big difference.

Of course they are not always angels, so if they are being too talkative in class then we might reach up for our 'silence sparkles'. They get to grab the sparkles from the sky and when it comes over their shoulders, that's when they need to be quiet. Or if they are talking too loud, I'll go really quiet and whisper which calms them immediately.

Very few Dance Studio Owners can operate a partnership as successfully as our next featured guests. Amanda and Lisette have together built a phenomenal business both in their recreational and intensive program. It's a rare delight to see two business-women and great friends who are able to capitalize on their strengths for the greater good of the business.

Amanda Hunsley and Lisette Stein are the owners of Prestige Dance Academy in Alberta, Canada.

Since opening Prestige in 2002, with the singular goal of sharing the love of dance, Amanda Hunsley is known for her passion, innovation, and kindness. Amanda motivates and inspires students, employees, and small business owners throughout Calgary.

Amanda holds a degree in Applied Business and Entrepreneurship from Mount Royal College. She has completed level two of the National Coaching Certification Program, and is also a certified teacher through the Associated Dance Arts for Professional Teachers (ADAPT) program.

Lisette Stein is the co-owner and artistic director of Prestige Dance Academy. She is well known for her insightful, innovative and masterful choreography which has won numerous awards both locally and internationally.

In 2017, Lisette was named Jazz Director for Team Canada, and led the team to gold in Poland at the World Dance Championships. This amazing success has brought her back to the choreography panel in 2019.

Lisette lives in Calgary, Alberta, Canada with her husband, Keith, and her loving dog, Toby.

Check out Amanda and Lisette's latest studio news at prestigedance.com

Chapter Ten

CHANGING LIVES THROUGH INNOVATION: AMANDA & LISETTE

Prestige Dance Academy Inc.

YOU TOOK ON A LOT OF RISK OPENING YOUR STUDIO – CAN YOU TELL US ABOUT YOUR EARLY DAYS AND HOW YOU GOT STARTED?
Amanda: We opened in August of 2002. We both grew up dancing at the same studio and both have different backgrounds. I have a business degree Lisette has a Bachelor of Fine Arts, with a major in theater and a minor in dance, as well as all of our dance training.

In 2002, I opened the studio and I was just turning 18 that year. My parents lent me money and co-signed the lease that essentially said if I was a failure, they would lose their home.

The rest is history. We're entering our 18th year, and it's been just growing and growing.

Lisette came on as a partner a bit further down the track. I was looking for a teacher for a Saturday morning. Really quickly after that, it was obvious that she was really good at what she does.
Lisette: I was still in university at the time. I was 19 and wanted to be a playwright and had no interest in being a teacher at all. But I knew Amanda from dance and when she asked, I thought, why not? Saturday morning job for a couple of hours sounds great. I was being trained to become a dance teacher and it was something that I wanted to have

behind me just because I loved dance. I really had no intention of actually pursuing it as a career until I started teaching for Amanda, and then found that I really fell in love with the connection and the children and teaching.

Amanda: Lisette joined the team in 2005 and it just grew. In 2014 we were planning to open a second location so she bought in as a partner in the business since then and now we work together all the time. Nothing's really changed that much, other than it's great having a partner. We're very lucky to have each other to work through the ups and downs of owning a business and the ups and downs of the dance studio.

HOW DO YOU SPLIT WHAT YOU DO AS BUSINESS PARTNERS? DO YOU HAVE SET ROLES, AND HOW DO YOU BALANCE THAT WITH THE TWO OF YOU GETTING EVERYTHING DONE?

Lisette: Amanda had already entrusted me with a lot of responsibility in running the day-to-day classes, and what we call the Intensive Program, which is a competitive program. It is one of the biggest in our area and quite successful and a huge part of our identify as a studio.

My title is the Artistic Director and Amanda is the Business Director.

Amanda does more of the day-to-day operational business side of it, with our bookkeeping staff, and she does most of the forward thinking in regards to business expansion. I still do a lot of the organizing of the artistic development of the classes and the competition program and inspiring our teachers.

WHAT ARE THE LESSONS YOU ARE IMPARTING THROUGHOUT YOUR INTENSIVE PROGRAM FOR FUTURE DANCERS AND INDUSTRY LEADERS?

Lisette: If we're talking about a future in dance or a career in dance, the first thing that they need to have is grit. It's something that is very important in any career you choose or in your life in general. It's a very hard industry and we need to ensure that the children understand that not everybody is a star all the time, and you're not always going to get all the jobs that you want.

In order to have a successful career in the industry, you need to make sure that grit is the first and foremost thing that you do have. It's usually not the most talented dancers that are the ones that are actually working in the industry, it is the ones that are the hardest workers. I find a lot of the time, it's actually the most talented ones that end up not dancing because they find that they don't have that grit.

I worry that's becoming an epidemic that our younger generation is going through right now, especially when we have competitions that are giving trophies for not placing, for example. We've created that mentality, so to bring back the idea of grit is essential to make sure that they are successful in this journey.

The other thing I always talk to them about is the need to be a triple threat. Sometimes in a very contemporary and lyrical driven dance world, right now especially, we need to ensure that they have an acting background, that they have a singing background, that they know how to tap, that they know how to do acro, that they know how to partner.

All of those things are really essential to them receiving roles and understanding that they are not going to be doing 85 pirouettes in an audition. They might be asked to do eight walks. How do you sell those walks? So often we focus so much on the technique, we forget about the actual acting and performing component for our senior dancers.

The last one I would say is just to be a team player. People want to work with people that are easy to work with, and really focusing on contributing and sharing ideas. We do a lot of that with the children, getting them to think for themselves and create for themselves, so that when they go for auditions, they are not necessarily going to be given set choreography. They will be asked to create work and show what makes them different. They need to know how to think for themselves and contribute ideas. That's a big part of being a team player: contributing.

Amanda: Likeability is also a big thing. You could be the most amazing dancer, but you've got the worst attitude and that's not just in dance, that's in life.

Lisette: There are a lot of businesses now that do likeability tests to find out if you are going to really be cohesive in this industry with this certain group of people.

WHAT MAKES YOUR INTENSIVE PROGRAM SO SUCCESSFUL?

Lisette: We have a very dedicated group of teachers that are invested beyond their job description, which is very important. We've just been blessed to have that connection, and relationships are so much of what

I believe makes our intensive program successful and our studio in general.

We have very talented staff members that work for us and children that are very dedicated and trust those teachers. We work really hard and have very high expectations of ourselves and have embedded that in our students.

Amanda: We want our teachers to pursue all the educational opportunities that they can. We also show them in different ways how much we value them. That connection between the staff and us really does create that loyalty, which is very important. We try to accommodate their needs. If one of them wants to pursue a direction of the studio that they want to expand on, we would encourage that because we want to give them the freedom to fulfill what they are passionate about.

Like Lisette, for example. When we knew how great she was as the intensive teacher, it just made sense that she pursue becoming the intensive director. We are very aware of doing that for all of our staff, because we feel like if they have the opportunity and you empower them to take the lead on things, they really rise to our expectations.

Lisette: We really empower our staff. We have to. We're up to three locations now within the city and we have big dreams beyond that, and we can't do it by ourselves. They really respond to being empowered and being trusted to do what they want to do. Then they feel like it's 'their baby' and will continue to strive for that excellence.

WHAT ARE YOUR TOP FOUR TIPS FOR SOCIAL MEDIA SUCCESS?

Amanda: We turned the corner to really be leading in terms of that when we decided we needed to hire a professional to help us with the photos and the videos because we were trying to do it. We needed to take it to the next level so that it wasn't just a dance studio, it was a more professional look. The photos and videos, they have to be professional and they have to look amazing, because they are representing your business. We have ours done by professionals so we couldn't go back now.

Videos have been essential to our growth. We've always been apprehensive, because in some ways I feel we don't want to be bragging about the success of the children or how strong they are, but it's also important to share what they've accomplished so people see what we do.

Empire Media Worx, which has done all of our professional videos, has completely set us apart from all of the businesses around us, from just a professional standard. We work at a professional standard, even though we are an amateur studio. Our goals are always professional standard goals.

Lisette: Next is having innovative and modern ideas. We're always trying to think outside the box and be who we are. Everything that goes on our social media is planned out and thought out. We try and make our photos and videos emotionally captivating, so that you want people to love the video. Even people have said to us, they wanted to watch that video over and over and it gave them goosebumps. Making sure that you emotionally captivate people to think, *Wow, that's beautiful. I want my child to dance at their dance studio.*

Make sure you're showcasing the diversity at the studio. We showcase our recreational program, our intensive program, our sessional programs, so we try and make sure we're doing all of that, within our social media posts.

WHAT QUALITIES MAKE YOU SUCCESSFUL LEADERS IN THIS COMPETITIVE INDUSTRY?

Amanda: We're always growing as leaders and every time we get to a good point, we learn to be even better.

Lisette: We're very transparent and relatable as leaders, and very honest. That's something that our staff relates to and that we can then feel more related to. Even to our staff and clients we've often said, "You know what? We don't have all the answers all the time. We are not going to pretend that we do, but we are going to figure it out the best way we can."

That's really allowed our staff to feel like they can have a transparent relationship with us and feel like they can be vulnerable and come to us with different things, because we work very much on the ground level with them and understand them.

If our staff was describing me, I think they would say that I can inspire people to produce good work and to not settle for anything less than what they can do. And not because I necessarily demand it of them, but I'm very hard on myself personally and I have very high expectations, but people are excited to rise to those expectations.

When our students feel that they receive positive feedback from achieving the best they can do, it's absolutely worth it. And they are thankful that they've pushed themselves to that degree.

Amanda: Our team would describe me as organized, always trying to make sure everything that needs to be planned out is ready. Forward-thinking, always trying to make sure that we're on the leading edge and being very open. We communicate a lot. We probably over-communicate, but it really works for us. We typically know how each other are feeling about things and support each other in our ideas and dreams. Sometimes I'll suggest something that might not be exactly what Lisette would be considering, but she would support me if she felt that I thought I was really passionate about it and that's exactly the same thing. If she comes to me with an idea of something that's inspiring her, we 100% support each other.

We do the same with our staff. We're very loyal to each other, to our clients, to our people who work for us. We respect everyone who works for us very much and we treat everybody the way we would want to be treated. If we do something wrong, we just own it and we don't pretend that we're perfect. We apologize, we make things right. We try to be very fair.

Sometimes we move children down levels or take children out of things, or we make a big drastic change, and that can be so hard. We always put the childs best interest at the front of our mind, always. Sometimes we make those tough decisions for that. Then we can justify it because it's in the best interests of the children, then we know we're doing it for the right reason.

Above all, we hold high professional standards for our staff and for the education of our students.

WHAT DO YOU DO IN YOUR BUSINESS TO ENSURE YOUR IDEAL CLIENTS KEEP COMING BACK EACH SEASON?

Amanda: It's about connection, and relationships. The dancers who have showed up on our doorstep at two years old and graduate at 18, that's because of relationships and human connection.

We truly care about these children. For example, our students that graduated last year, we sent them care packages to their college dorms. They are no longer clients, we have nothing to gain from them financially, but we want to show them that their relationship with us did go beyond that of just being clients.

We get invited to their graduations; they get four tickets to graduation, and we're sitting there next to mom and dad. That's how we keep them and it's from a real and sincere place.

Lisette: We use the Inner Circle onboarding process to make that connection right away. We have sent flowers to our clients when parents pass away, we write cards. We just make sure that we go above and beyond all the time because that's what we would want, too.

When I'm dealing with other businesses and I'm the client, I often think, *What did they do wrong here? And what am I doing wrong in my business? How could I have made this a different call and left my client with a happier experience?*

A big part of it is being introspective and going above and beyond all the time, and making it about more than just dance. It means so much to us that they continue to come to our business year after year. We do value them and we do want them to be treated the way we would want to be treated.

Amanda: We also ask for a lot of feedback. When someone brings us their feedback, we want to use it to help make us better because we'd rather someone come and talk to us about what they feel we could do better. Then learn from it and grow our business in a better way.

It's a pleasure to share this Dance Studio CEO's journey with you, because she is so passionate about sharing her knowledge and experience. Jodi's commitment to sharing her expertise and lifting up her team members is a huge inspiration and asset to our community. She was one of our first Inner Circle members and I know you're going to love her story.

Jodi Shilling is the CEO of Relevé Studios in California, USA.

She is a Dance Performance graduate from Oklahoma City University and recipient of the 2008 OCU Distinguished Alumni Award and continues to enjoy working in film and television as well.

Jodi's dance and choreography credits include: Natalie Cole Live tour, Timber Lake Playhouse, choreographer for numerous promotional events and theatre companies in the New York, Chicago, and Los Angeles areas.

On television, Jodi has been seen as: 4th season recurring guest star Tiffany on The Disney Channel's *That's So Raven*, Robin on Disney's *Hannah Montana*, Jessica on Comedy Central's *Laughs4Life* with Steve Carell (season 1) and Stephen Colbert (season 2), Kessler on TV Land's *I Did Not Know That* with Harry Shearer, a series regular on *Betty and DD*, as well as several indie movies, including a faith-based comedy, *Can I Get a Witness Protection*.

Her performance credits also include numerous commercials, radio spots, animated voices, industrials, and over 50 stage-productions.

Jodi is married to her hilarious husband of 19 years and has two young daughters, Pixie (age five), and Whimsy (age three). She loves to travel, cook, create art, live life joyously, and is completely obsessed with dogs.

Check out Jodi's latest studio news at relevestudios.com

Chapter Eleven

KEEPING YOUR DANCERS FOR A LIFETIME: JODI SHILLING

Relevé Studios

YOU HAD A VERY EXCITING CAREER AS A PERFORMER BEFORE YOU OPENED YOUR STUDIO – CAN YOU TELL US ABOUT YOUR JOURNEY FROM ONSTAGE-ROMANCE, TO DISNEY TV STAR AND FINALLY TO RELEVÉ STUDIOS CEO?

I was trained as a dancer and immediately after college I was hired as an actress. It was a fluke, because it was a summer stock call for musical theater. I had never sung, I had never acted, and I had to do all three things. To compensate for my lack of singing ability I made some jokes and made the audience laugh.

I continued with my monologue and made the audience laugh some more. By the time they got to the dance call, they didn't even care if I could dance because it had turned into a comedic show and I got hired for Timber Lake Playhouse just outside Chicago for my first professional play. It so happens, that's where I met my husband, Shon. He was playing the lead opposite character and we were supposed to fall in love in the play. Then it happened in real life.

My mom was in the audience and after the show she just knew. Three months later, he proposed and we moved to New York where I started my acting career before my agent sent us to Los Angeles. Eventually, about three years into auditioning and working in that way, I hit it big on a Disney show called *That's So Raven*. Once that contract had ended, I finally had the capital and I opened up my studio with my Disney money. I had a little bit of a following because of the character I played and was able to start my dream studio in 2008.

We named it Relevé Studios.

Actually my husband named it because he said that I am so uplifting and so encouraging, we should have a studio that means to rise up. The rest is history.

WHAT HAVE YOU TAKEN FROM YOUR PROFESSIONAL CAREER AS A PERFORMER THAT HELPS YOU RUN RELEVÉ?

The key to my success as a performer has been the ability to say, "Yes, I can do that" – even if I really couldn't at the time. I had to always be open-minded and confident in extending myself and learning new things. Another huge factor was to have very well-rounded training in all styles of dance.

Eventually I did get voice lessons, and acting, and it's really, really opened up the possibilities for myself, and I pass that on to our dancers.

They train across the board, in every performing arts genre there is, and we expose them both to film and video work, along with stage work. In that way, it's had a huge influence on how I operate.

HOW MANY HOURS DO YOU SPEND TEACHING IN YOUR STUDIO?

That's evolved. When I first opened, I was teaching between 20-25 hours a week, and it wasn't sustainable.

Then I shaved off about five hours each year. This year I am teaching two classes each week, and I plan to teach nothing next year which is hard, but it's necessary because it allows me to oversee everything that's going on.

I can always step in and assist or sub, but no regular, weekly classes for me next year.

WHAT DO YOU CONSIDER HAVE BEEN THE THREE BIGGEST MILESTONES IN YOUR CAREER THAT REALLY PUNCTUATE THE JOURNEY YOU'VE BEEN ON TO TRANSITION FROM A HOBBY-BUSINESS TO A GO-TO DANCE STUDIO?

The first major one was not one that I ever wanted or expected, but it really hit me when I lost my first born daughter, and then I lost my mom shortly after that.

Then I had a second child, and that was all within two years.

I couldn't cope and I had to leave. When my mom was fighting cancer, I left my studio purposely in the hands of my studio manager, because family first, always. I just couldn't be spending time or energy there. I will always stand by the decision I made of course, but when I did leave we found out the hard way whether my systems were working or not.

Some of them were, and some of them weren't, so that was a huge, huge milestone for me, because it was very eye-opening to where the studio sat in the grand scheme of my life. It's very, very important, but it's not the most important thing. Up until that point, I may have put it on a pedestal.

That was the first milestone.

Through that, I allowed my dance studio community to engulf me, especially after I lost my daughter. That really bonded us. People saw the values of my family and other community, like my church community. It was just an extraordinary thing.

We developed a memorial dance scholarship fund in honor of my daughter Daisy, and that's about the time I reached out and found the Dance Studio Owners Inner Circle, which really paved the way for the next four years of growth. I owe so much to you, and the Inner Circle.

I would say the next milestone was when I realized I needed to invest in my staff and teachers, and continue my own education, and pass that on to them. So, the next milestone was the evolvement of my managerial skills, and team-building, and leadership, and setting in stone retreat dates to educate the staff, and then even the students and assistants.

My final milestone has been the financial piece.

When I stepped away from my business, it caused havoc on my finances, because when the leader steps away from the helm of the ship, it can keep sailing a straight course, but there's no one there to make it turn if it needs to turn, or change directions. And so there was zero growth, and maybe just a little bit of loss.

Financially, I had to really, really pull it together and make some changes when I came back, to get it back in the healthy position. Knowing and understanding my numbers took a lot of time, but was so worth it and invaluable in getting back on track.

WHAT WOULD YOUR TEAM SAY IT IS LIKE TO WORK WITH YOU?
I asked my team this recently.

The first one said I was their mentor, and I loved that.

The second person said they described me as uplifting, which I also loved because that is the entire mission of this studio.

The third person said I was a 'velvet hammer'. And that is actually a name that I knew was going around about me, but basically, his point is that I can bring down the law, but it's like velvet. I'm still not sure if that's a good thing!

OTHER THAN THAT INITIAL DISNEY APPEAL, WHAT HAVE BEEN SOME OF YOUR BEST STUDENT ATTRACTION STRATEGIES?
The Disney thing only worked for 15 minutes. You know what they say, you get 15 minutes of fame!

One of the main things is, we are highly involved in the local schools in our area, teaching throughout the day, musical theater, acting, and dance. That has positioned us as an authority in our community, so we tend to be one of the first places people come when they have noticed that their child has a desire to take it even further outside of school, then they come to our studio. So that would be number one.

Number two has been the involvement of developing my online marketing skills. We use Facebook Ads and Google AdWords consistently, every week, and we spend quite a bit of money on it.

Then the third thing is a strong referral program. It's even better than the first two. The referrals are always our best. The best people come in from the referrals, because they are a great cultural fit and are just like the students you already have and love.

We have these cards that we hand out which are a 'One Week Class Pass'. Our dancers can grab as many as they want, and then they hand out the one week passes to friends and family. If a student comes in with the pass, and it has the name of the person who gave it to them on it, the person who gave it gets $20.

If the referral actually signs up, they get $20 credit towards their first month. They usually come in and try some of our classes in that week, and they usually end up taking a couple.

WHAT IS THE BEST ADVICE THAT YOU RECEIVED?

'We don't live to work – we work so that we can live.' That's the best advice I've ever gotten.

The second-best advice, and what has transformed my last couple of years and made it possible for me to relocate, to buy a house, to buy a car, and all these things I never thought would happen is this: It's because I've decided to spend the top 80% of my time is in the top 20% of what I should be doing.

That 20% is acquiring big account leads, working on visionary tasks, and a little bit of team-building – that's where I spend my time.

It was tough to apply at first, because I couldn't do it until I had the right team. I now have an office manager and five staff dedicated to the office who cover all that admin work so that it frees me up to do the things that I need to do.

It was scary every time I would hire a new person, because I would think to myself, *How am I going to pay?* But then when I'm spending the time on the things that are bringing in more money, that more than pays for the new hire.

WHO ARE YOUR TOP ROLE MODELS IN BUSINESS, AND WHY?

A major inspiration is Jo Rowan and John Bedford from Oklahoma City University, which was my alma mater. They were one of the first schools to start an American dance program that incorporated jazz, and tap, and ballet, and all of the different styles, because for most of the universities, it was only ballet and modern.

When we went through that school, we had opportunities to do voice, and theater, and dance – they made all these options available.

Even dance management classes, and real live projects, like creating your own production. They were one of the first to really educate in that way, and a lot of the practices that I've learned there, I have applied in my life and continue to pass on to my students. The way they set up that program is absolutely brilliant, and I have huge admiration and gratefulness towards them.

Next, I would say it would be my father, Jerry Shilling. He started a business out of our living room when I was just a baby, and it was a criss-cross grid where rain, and soil, and dirt could fall through, but the grass would still grow. It was really easy to clean, because you would just hose it off. He had been a farmer, and he invented this livestock flooring, and then turned it into outdoor furniture.

Throughout my life, this business started in his living room, and then grew to this international company. He ended up selling it when I had just graduated from college. He's enjoyed this long, lengthy retirement, and I get the best advice from him regarding business and growth.

I would also say my faith plays a huge role in business, and how I operate. We are by no means a Christian dance studio, but the values are there in my dealings and business, and how I treat others, and the rulebook that I live by.

YOU'RE IN A VERY CULTURALLY DIVERSE AREA OF LOS ANGELES – CAN YOU GIVE US A SNAPSHOT OF WHAT THIS LOOKS LIKE IN YOUR STUDIO?

It's amazing, we have Hindu, Muslim, Jewish, Christian students – and many religions in between! Christianity is the minority, and it's so interesting and uplifting to have Hindu, Islam and Jewish all training and dancing by the same values in the same studio.

As far as ethnicities, you name it, we have it. And where the studio is located, we're right smack in between a very wealthy neighborhood, and a very low socio-economic neighborhood. So our classroom is, in every way imaginable, completely diverse. I wouldn't have it any other way, and it shows not only in our marketing, but in the styles of dance we offer.

We offer salsa, Cha-cha, and all the Latin styles. We offer Bollywood, African, hula, Irish. There's a lot of sub-genres we offer, because of the neighborhood that we are in. I love it. I have learned so much.

HOW ARE YOU PREPARING YOUR DANCERS FOR THEIR FUTURES, EITHER IN OR OUTSIDE OF THE PERFORMING ARTS INDUSTRY?

One thing I have noticed in the training of dancers is that dancers these days are accomplishing extraordinary feats, and technical skills. Some of them, I am not sure are appropriate for the age of the children who are performing them, and the amount of hours and training it takes to get there as a child, I'm not necessarily in agreement with.

So, one thing that is separating our studio from other studios is that it's vital that we take the whole child approach, because I think that it will hurt them as adults, or even teens, if we push them too hard as children.

I don't believe we have any students dancing more than 12 hours, and that, to me, is even a little too much a week. We put high emphasis on schooling. We have homework stations and tutoring available at the studio, but if a child falls behind in school, the parent can come to us, and we will put a hold on their tuition.

Another thing is, if they need to break for any sort of family event, or a wedding, or whatever it is, we don't penalize in our teams. Our competition teams like that, we are not that strict as far as what we're asking the families, as far as commitment, and time.

We may not be as technically-focused as some other studios in our area, but we are teaching our children how to grow, and we're taking it in the right incremental steps. We are trying to make sure that they are really well-rounded in all areas of their lives. Socially, mentally, intellectually, and then also physically in dance. It really sets us apart.

I have been so impressed with our next featured Studio Owner's growth as she has transformed into the CEO of her studio. It's been a pleasure and a privilege to witness her make a lot of big-picture decisions over the last 12 months and her persistence and resilience has been an inspiration to everyone around her.

Kim is the founder and principal teacher at Centre Stage Studio in Thetford, England. Her background in teaching has helped her to create a studio built on strong values, that is known for its inclusion and consideration of the whole student.

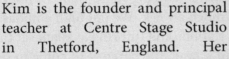

She trained in the north east and gained her dance teaching qualifications with the N.B.D.O. and then qualified with the I.D.T.A. a few years later. Prior to opening the studio she gained her Postgraduate Certificate in Education with early years specialism and taught as a primary school teacher for six years. Here she was graded 'outstanding' by Ofsted and was a lead teacher in Norfolk for early years teaching. Kim also has a Bachelor of Science degree in Psychology.

She is married and lives with her husband Tim, who is also the preschool programs manager at the studio. In her spare time Kim likes to be by the coast, visits family and enjoys the odd spa day! She is also involved in helping the homeless in her local community.

Check out Kim's latest studio news at centrestageschoolofdance1.com

Chapter Twelve

STANDING OUT AS THE GO-TO DANCE STUDIO: KIM RITCHIE

Centre Stage School of Dance

CAN YOU TELL US ABOUT YOUR TRANSITION FROM DANCE TEACHER TO DANCE STUDIO OWNER?

I started quite late into the dance world, I was 11 when I started which is quite late. There was a studio across the road from me and one day I just decided – I'm going dancing with my pocket money. I absolutely loved it, and as I got older I helped my dance teacher here and there by teaching and assisting, but my goal in life was to be a psychologist.

I got into university and as part of my degree I also needed to study education, and I absolutely loved it. I loved being a teacher and I was also naturally quite good at it. I got a job in a school and wanted to offer dance in the area because there wasn't much around, so I did an after school club on a Tuesday night for the children.

Eventually a couple of parents from the after school club kept asking if they could join my dance school. I didn't even have one, but I knew there was something there so I started my little dance school and the rest is history.

UNITED KINGDOM DANCE SCHOOLS ARE QUITE UNIQUE COMPARED WITH THE USA OR CANADA – WHAT DOES THE 'STUDIO SCENE' LOOK LIKE IN YOUR AREA?

Firstly, it's very rare to have your own premises here. I'm very lucky that I do, but I didn't start off that way. Dance schools tend to operate out of hiring school halls and church halls, so you've got to fit round their availability. Having your own building is a very rare luxury.

WHAT DRIVES YOU IN BUSINESS?

The whole reason that I started up really is because in the town where I am, there weren't a lot of opportunities for children to dance. I wanted to provide a place that was accessible for all, but still very good quality.

I've learned a few lessons along the way, but what drives me is still just making it accessible for all. Allowing everyone to be involved. We are more than just dance now – we offer musical theater, drama, acro, and they can come and do it all under one roof.

It's all about the students. It doesn't matter if they are not the best dancer in the world, I'd much rather they were kind, friendly, and gained confidence and that's the biggest drive. We're more than just coming to the studio and achieving distinction in exams. We spend time chatting about life, school, and getting to know the students personally. Especially these days, children are stressed out and they need somewhere to let off steam. Dance and the performing arts is one of the best ways to do this.

WHO DO YOU LOOK UP TO?

My dance teacher Pauline is a huge inspiration. She was my only dance teacher and she did a lot for me. When the studio moved I couldn't get there anymore so I went to her house and she drove me to class. I stayed and she drove me back again. When I couldn't pay for my costumes she allowed me to come and do some work in the shop to pay it off that way. She always went above and beyond, so I have taken that attitude into my own studio, and today in the studio if we can help we will. We do try our best to make people feel welcomed and valued, and she has had a big impact on how I run things.

My mom is also a wonderful role model, I was always told whatever you want to do, you can do it. They support me, whether I was going to be a bin-man or a doctor, it didn't matter. Whatever I wanted to be, whatever I wanted to do, I had unconditional support to do it. I've got quite a drive because of that. Whatever I want to do, I know I'll get there somehow.

People in Dance Studio Owners Inner Circle are huge inspirations. I see what they have achieved and their journeys and think, *I want to be like them when I grow up!*

YOU'VE BEEN OPEN FOR EIGHT YEARS NOW – WHAT HAS CHANGED IN THE BUSINESS LANDSCAPE DURING THAT TIME?

It would be the social media influence, and pressures on the students and parents as well. The quick gratification and instant results that are going up on YouTube and Instagram is quite tricky to combat. But that's why it is so important as a studio to teach children that it takes a long time to learn skills and if you keep going and persevere, you will get there.

We have a set of values and one of them is perseverance so we talk a lot about this. We turn social media around so that it can work for us, not against us. We put up lots of posts about technique; we do lots of videos and we are very clear about the fact that they have learnt this as a foundation. It's important to show that we know what we are talking about.

We advertise about our expertise a lot as well to show that we've got teachers here who are going to make sure the children are safe. We are honest with the children about it too, and if they start trying DIY tricks or YouTube tutorials, we say "You can do that, but let's try and make it better so that it's going to keep your body safe in the future" and they understand that. They see it's not a personal attack.

WHAT ARE YOUR STUDIO'S SUPERPOWERS?

Definitely our values. We've really focused on these, and we tweak them all the time and talk about them all the time as a team.

We hire with those values

too. All of our interview questions are based around the values that we have so that we know we are going to get people who believe and agree with our studio culture. Our whole team are definitely very involved in all our goals and mission.

My husband Tim and I are both in management roles in the studio and we both have very strong early years teaching backgrounds, which gives us quite a unique perspective. Tim's role is to also help and support the teachers at that age too, so that's been amazing. As a trained teacher he can give some perspective and really help in the classroom in areas like behavior management or class structures where a lot of dance teachers may struggle.

HOW DO YOU SPLIT THE ROLES WHEN WORKING WITH YOUR SPOUSE TO AVOID ANY TENSION OR 'STUDIO FATIGUE'?

We've always worked together – we both taught at the same primary school, so working together is luckily very natural for us and we love it. We are both trained in the early years background, and having an under-sevens program in the studio had been a goal of mine for about a year, but I just never got round to it.

It was never happening, getting in classes and monitoring and changing, building the curriculum etc. I felt like I had this big goal that I didn't have time to do. He finished teaching his job at the same time I was going to look for somebody and I said, "This is perfect for you, if you want this role."

Now he looks after all the under-sevens department. He is managing assessments, creating curriculum, and supporting our teachers. He is improving all of our communication as well because parents want to

be more involved, they weren't sure what was going on, what the children were doing in class, so he's taken that role on and he's making sure parents are more involved.

We've started parent participation weeks now, so they are coming in at the studio and seeing what's going on. There are more regular newsletters, it's been great having him there and taking on really separate roles in the studio.

DO YOU HAVE ANY BIG 'A-HA' MOMENTS THAT HAVE CHANGED THE WAY YOU RUN YOUR BUSINESS?

I guess the biggest one was you can't do it all alone. I did it on my own for a good few years and didn't grow.

Then it was reading *Dance Studio Transformation* that I realized I've just got to take the plunge and hire people and get help. I've got no qualms whatsoever about doing that anymore. If you want to get better, if you want to grow and you want to impact more people in the dance world then you need to get help. Success isn't working 24/7. You haven't got to be working all the time to prove that you're a hard worker and have got quite a strong work ethic – you need to take time out.

I do take more breaks now and I am more aware of when I need to stop and again that's all from the Dance Studio Owners Inner Circle and their impact on that. I just enjoy life more now. I do find it a little bit easier to switch off. I still find that a bit tricky, but you can't just keep running on empty all the time. The biggest thing was the fact that it's not any good for your studio or your staff, so actually by thinking you need to be in there and keep working, you're creating a negative impact for everybody else around you.

If you're an altruistic person, you can just think of it that way. You're not being helpful to anybody by just plowing on through. It's all right to take a break and definitely helps productivity and gets your mojo back.

Another big lesson for me has been that you can't please everybody. Stop trying to please everybody.

HOW WOULD YOU DESCRIBE YOURSELF AS THE CEO OF YOUR BUSINESS?

I'd like to think that I am firm but fair. I do have high expectations but I am also realistic and very honest. Something that's been added into our values very recently actually is honesty and integrity.

I just want my staff to be the best they can be, enjoy their time while they are at work whilst still providing top class service and the two of them go hand-in-hand. If they love being there and want to do well and feel valued then they are going to provide the best they can be.

In a training we had recently, the last hour and forty-five minutes was about them and what are your goals. I didn't want them talk about work – I wanted to know what do they want to get out of life. What do they want to do, and if I can help I will. If you want to go to Hawaii I'm sorry I can't help with that one, but if it's to take a course, or more time out I can do what I can to accommodate that.

One of my staff members goals was to go on a date night once a month with her husband and I can easily help with that.

WHAT HAVE BEEN THE BIGGEST LESSONS YOU HAVE LEARNED SINCE YOU OPENED YOUR DOORS EIGHT YEARS AGO THAT YOU WOULD LIKE TO PASS ON TO OUR FUTURE INDUSTRY LEADERS?

I've learnt so much, but I definitely accepted that without these people that I've hired, I wouldn't be where I am now and I have our recruitment process to thank for that. All of our questions at our interviews now are more valuable, we have probation periods, and it's just building that trust.

I would also definitely say that a huge lesson was in not taking everything personally. Let it go, that's definitely the way.

Take time out to meditate, and look after yourself.

Read the book *Profit First*. Make sure you're planning for the future. Put in place now what you think you're going to need in five or ten years' time and don't make expectations on things that are there now, because there's a lot of procedures that I wish I'd written down and put in place five or ten years ago. That would definitely be very useful. We've got a procedure queen now in our studio.

And find your tribe. Find the DSOA. Find a man called Clint Salter. Find them because my mental state since finding them is so different. The shift in how I think about things and how I take challenges and deal with challenges has just gone round in a full circle. There are people out there like you because you do feel very isolated as a studio owner, especially when you are starting out on your own with no help. If I had that support back then, I can't imagine where I would be now.

DANCE STUDIO SECRETS BONUS –
FIND OUT HOW KIM INCREASED HER OWN WAGE BY 20% IN
OUR EXCLUSIVE BONUS INTERVIEW AT
DSOA.COM/KIM

I am so proud of the woman you are going to meet next in Dance Studio Secrets. Marguerite has a wonderful, contagious energy and spirit. She is focused on building a fantastic business while also being focused on building a life by design. Marguerite is very intentional around building a fulfilling life for her and her family as well as running a successful business, which I believe is key to being an unstoppable CEO.

Marguerite Howlett is the CEO of The Renaissance School of Dance in Papatoetoe, New Zealand.

She teaches jazz, tap, hip hop, contemporary, and ballet dance styles. She has been dancing herself since she was three years old, doing exams, performing and choreographing in various events, including Santa parades, music videos, jubilees, Auckland Children's Musical Theatre, Manukau Performing Arts and City Dance Company.

She is also a dance consultant and program developer for local primary schools, preschools, after school care and holiday programs in Auckland.

Marguerite has completed exams in ballroom, Latin and new vogue, completed her visual arts degree from the University of Auckland and won 'Young Business Person of the Year 2008' at the Westpac Manukau Business Excellence Awards.

Feeding her love for travel she has competed across New Zealand, Australia, and the USA in modern jive and west coast swing events. Her favorite places to travel so far have been Fiji, San Francisco, Las Vegas, and Italy!

Check out Marguerite's latest studio news at renaissancedance. co.nz

Chapter Thirteen

CULTIVATING A LIFE BY DESIGN: MARGUERITE HOWLETT

The Renaissance School Of Dance

WHEN DID YOU DISCOVER YOUR PASSION FOR TEACHING DANCE?

My mom noticed that I was very much into dancing from a young age. So I started at two, she found some dance classes for me and I absolutely loved them. I loved being on stage and I loved dancing around the house all the time. When I was five years old I said, "I'm going to be just like my teacher one day, mom, when I grow up." And she laughed as you do with five year olds.

I kept dancing as a child and it was always my 'thing'. I really loved after school activities, so I was always trying to do everything and when it got a bit much and I had to drop something, I never dropped dance. Even when one of the dance schools that I went to closed down and I had to find another one. It wasn't an option to just leave it for a while. No, I needed to dance.

I went through a few different dance schools when I was younger and then continued as a teenager and that was throughout my studies in high school.

It was just those few hours a week that I could just relax and be myself. And then I'd go back to my studies again. I never quit or paused for any moment in time. When I was 17 my dance teacher asked if I wanted to start teaching some of her classes and of course I jumped at the chance because I loved little children and being a good role model for them. Then she started giving me more and more classes. She got pregnant and then she just lost interest in her dance studio.

A lot of the parents approached me asking, "Why don't you just start your own studio?" At first I just thought, *I can't do that. I'm only 18. What are you talking about?*

And then it kept nagging at me so l just started to teach a few classes to give me a bit of money on the side while I was at university. And it just grew from there.

It's why my studio is called The Renaissance School of Dance – 'renaissance' meaning rebirth. Now I've been running it for almost 15 years now and I've always had that same passion from when I started. I just wanted to dance, it's in my blood and I wanted to be a really good role model for the younger children and make them happy and share my passion of dance with them.

WHAT DOES THE DANCE STUDIO SCENE LOOK LIKE IN AUCKLAND RIGHT NOW?

We have about a million people in our city. I know you shouldn't compare, but I've got lots of dance studio owner friends in America and Australia, and comparatively New Zealand is just so tiny and Auckland is even tinier.

A lot of talented children who are finishing high school and university just don't see dance as a career. Actually, the whole country doesn't see dance as a career. We're more of a rugby nation, and anything in the arts is not very big.

But that's what I wanted to do, so I made it happen. I've just got that personality that I wanted to teach dance, so I teach dance. I made it full-time and I didn't make any excuses.

Most of the children who want a career in dance here in Auckland either have to teach, or they have to slog it out doing performances or creating their own choreography, but they still need another job on the side.

WHAT ARE THE TOP THREE THINGS THAT SET YOUR STUDIO APART FROM OTHERS IN YOUR AREA?

The first thing is definitely family and inclusivity. We just have this real vibe in the studio that everyone is welcome. We have new students starting year round and we welcome them with open arms. We have policies and procedures in place on how to welcome a new student and get them included in the class as soon as possible. We really celebrate diversity, that everybody has something to give or everybody has something that they are good at or that they can contribute to the world.

Also that we try and make things as easy as possible for parents. They don't have to do the hair and makeup for the children for performances or shows. We do that for them. We do all the costuming for them. So when it comes to our big end of the year show, the parents will literally just drop the child off, go sit in the audience, have a little cry at how amazing it is and then come pick the child up.

It's super chill and laid back, which is the essence of what our country and culture is about here in New Zealand.

We're also really big on customer service, the customer experience and communicating. We're very open and transparent.

WHO ARE YOUR ROLE MODELS IN BUSINESS, AND WHY?

One of my huge passions is reading and I read at least a book a week. I remember one of the very first audiobooks that I listened to was Tim Ferriss' *The 4-Hour Work Week* and now I follow a lot of his stuff.

Also when I first started hiring staff, I had a few issues so I started following Richard Branson and one of the things he says is if you look after your employees, they will look after your clients. A few years ago I made it my big project to focus on my people, the people that work for me. And in turn, obviously they've now looked after the people who come to our studio.

And Clint Salter and the Dance Studio Owners Inner Circle has absolutely changed my business.

WHAT OTHER THINGS DO YOU LOVE TO DO OUTSIDE OF YOUR BUSINESS TO STAY BALANCED?

If you had asked me a few years ago, I would have said nothing! I didn't do anything outside of my studio because I've always been so super career focused and that was what I loved to do.

Then I discovered traveling with my partner, and we love to learn about different cultures and travel across the world. When I fell pregnant and I thought, *Oh, okay, this is going to change a bit*. It's really changed in a good and very big way. He was the cutest little kid and I absolutely love being a mom, so in the last few years I've made more of a conscious effort to not only balance, but I don't spend as much time in the studio anymore because I've also developed the studio to run by itself most of the time.

Now I do so much outside the studio because I don't need to worry about it.

I play with my little boy. We do loads of activities together. He's almost two, but I love sharing the world with him. I'm a very passionate reader and like playing board games, hanging out with my partner, my friends, and traveling, which I can do running the business because I can leave for a week or two.

WHAT ARE SOME OF THE BIGGEST CHANGES YOU HAVE SEEN IN OUR INDUSTRY OVER THE LAST 15 YEARS IN BUSINESS?

There's a huge lack of commitment these days. We just get so busy and often, especially with the younger children. Parents have an attitude of, "Oh we'll just try it for a term (eight to ten weeks) and see how we go." Here in New Zealand and Australia the year is split up into four terms, and we have holidays in between each term.

We have so many holidays and children drop off during those times. It's one thing I am going to change. What if dancing keeps going year round? I'm going to try it out next year.

Another thing that has changed is social media and the way we communicate and everything on the Internet. Social media is how I communicate with the parents, but also on the flip-side there is the whole Instagram thing where children are looking at what other children can do but not seeing all the effort or all the back story. Sure, that's a great picture but you don't see what's happened behind it. Or they might not even go to a dance studio at all – they could just be at home trying to figure it out for themselves.

We are really trying to instill those values in children while celebrating what we do in our studio, knowing that everybody has something to give and you don't have to be the best at everything.

WHAT ARE SOME OF THE 'A-HA' MOMENTS THAT HAVE SHAPED YOUR STUDIO?

The first one was having my son. I wasn't expecting to love being a mom because I was so career focused and work focused.

Another big moment that was earlier this year where we experienced a few tragedies in my life and a few loved ones passed away within the space of a month. My partner and I had a big discussion about our life values and how we want to be remembered, and what legacy we want to leave. After that, we don't have a house anymore. We've become professional house sitters, which means that we can travel around a lot more. We've changed our life to be quite minimalist. We only have what we need. My project for the next year is to figure out how to run my business 100% away, off location so we're going to do lots more traveling because it's what we love.

One of our Inner Circle retreat speakers, Tina Tower has been a big inspiration in that area, and sharing how she formed the business before franchising and then selling it, and then traveling the world.

WHAT DO YOU THINK MIGHT BE HOLDING STUDIO OWNERS BACK FROM REACHING THEIR FULL POTENTIAL?

Mindset would be a huge one. Thinking too much about what people will think of them or just thinking too much at all. Not taking risks. Having your own business is risky but higher reward so you need to be willing to try new things. You have to try new things as an entrepreneur, as a business owner. You can't stand still. If you're standing still, you're not growing and if you're not growing, you're dying.

You always need to be doing something to make your customers happy or to make them go "Wow, that's why I'm part of this community."

And education, because I'm so big on reading and I'm part of the Dance Studio Owners Inner Circle. Education and being supported by other people who are going through the same thing is huge.

WHAT IS YOUR FAVORITE STUDENT ATTRACTION STRATEGY?

Because in our studio we're so inclusive and happy to have new students all the time and meeting new children and celebrating the differences between us all, word of mouth is a big one. And it's basically a lot of how my studio has grown.

We've also been really big on social media the last couple of years. Not necessarily 'sell, sell, sell' but just showcasing who we are, what we do, and what we love. We want to share that with our community.

IF YOU COULD GO BACK IN TIME AND GIVE YOURSELF ANY ADVICE WHEN YOU FIRST OPENED THE RENAISSANCE SCHOOL OF DANCE, WHAT WOULD THE ADVICE BE?

First of all would be to get your finances in check right from day one. Set up systems for accounting, and be really strict with the finances, checking your profit and loss statement because that's my weakness. And I keep putting it off, all the other pillars in my studio were holding themselves up. But that is the one that kept crumbling and falling.

The other thing is to join support networks. So I joined local network groups when I was younger and I found that quite frustrating, because they didn't understand how dance studios work and the passion and drive behind it. Joining things like the Dance Studio Owners Association with other dance studio owners, and not necessarily teachers. There's a big difference between being a teacher and being a studio owner or business owner. I've enjoyed that transition.

DANCE STUDIO SECRETS BONUS –
GRAB MARGUERITE'S PROVEN 11-STEP ENROLLMENT PROCESS AND SAY GOODBYE TO STUDENT ENQUIRIES SLIPPING THROUGH THE CRACKS AT
DSOA.COM/MARGUERITE

It's not every day that you meet a husband and wife team who work as cohesively as our next featured Studio Owners, Kendra and Chris. This pair are in tune with their strengths within their partnership and they are both so passionate about their roles inside of the studio. Their ability to come together to make the studio an extraordinary place for their parents and their students and the care that they put into training and nurturing their team is second to none.

Kendra Slatt is the founder and executive director of Perfect Pointe Music & Dance Studios. Ms Slatt is best known for her expertise in young children's programming and classical ballet, creating a strong culture of inclusivity, and for excellence in customer communication.

She holds a B.A. in Dance and a B.S. in Business Administration/Marketing from the State University of New York at Buffalo. She is a Certified Instructor of Rhythm Works Integrative Dance and also a graduate of the Dance Masters of America Teachers' Training School.

Together with husband Chris, a computer programmer-turned-dance studio business manager, she has grown Perfect Pointe from a one room dance studio into six dance studios, five private music studios and one group music/multi-purpose room, employing approximately 30 people and serving over 900 current students.

Chris and Kendra live with their two children in Arlington, VA. When not at the studio they enjoy long-distance bike riding, overly-complicated board games, and travel.

Check out Kendra and Chris' latest studio news at perfectpointe.com

Chapter Fourteen

PLANNING YOUR DANCE STUDIO EMPIRE: KENDRA & CHRIS SLATT

Perfect Pointe Music & Dance Studios

WHAT DREW YOU TO A CAREER AS A DANCE STUDIO OWNER?

Kendra: I started dancing when I was about five or six years old. My mom put me in class because she thought it would be good for me both as a physical activity and a social activity. It wasn't something that I had particularly asked for but she just thought it would be good for me and I ended up loving it. I loved my first teacher. I loved the structure of the ballet, the traditional ballet class until they started talking about recital that first year. I had this fear that people were going to look at me and I just said 'no'.

I wanted to drop out at that point and my mom just told me, "You're going to finish out the school year. We've committed to the year and it will be a good experience for you. If you really don't like it after you've finished out this year, then you don't have to sign up again next year. But I'm not just going to let you quit."

And I always thank her so much for doing that because imagine if I had quit halfway through my first year in dance how my life would be different today.

I survived my first recital and loved dance so much that I stuck with it. I've never really been a huge performer but loved the classroom work. When I was aged 11 or 12 one of my teachers asked me to be an assistant in the classroom with some preschool children. That's where I realized how much I loved working with the little ones and taking my analytical brain and being able to break things down and teach it to other people.

I come from a family of business people, so my brain has always been drawn to the business side of it as well. I would just constantly be thinking when I was going through in high school, *If I had my own studio, I would do it this way.* I always thought like that from a very young age.

By the time I was ready to graduate high school and starting to think about colleges, I already had that plan to open a studio. I just knew that that's what I wanted to do. I love the teaching part of it and I liked the business part of it, so I created my college plan around the idea of opening a dance studio.

WHAT ADVICE DO YOU HAVE FOR STUDIO OWNERS WHO STRIVE TO STAY INNOVATIVE IN BUSINESS?

Chris: I would say the most important thing is to take every new thing that comes along and really think critically about it. It's so easy when you're trying to be innovative and trying to evolve with the latest tech to jump onto every new thing that comes along and so often they just don't actually make sense for your business, or they don't make sense for the dance business in general.

I've felt that way about having a studio app for a very long time. We're finally getting to the point where maybe there is a business case there, but for so long it was just like your website but harder to use. That's the most important way to avoid making mistakes and trying to be innovative is to really think: what does this actually accomplish for my customers or my dancers?

WHAT ARE SOME OF THE PRODUCTIVITY TIPS AND TOOLS THAT YOU USE TO STAY ON TRACK AND FOCUSED EACH DAY?

Kendra: I'm a huge list person and so I just make myself lists. I organize my inbox into different folders and then have a system that works for me, of leaving certain things marked as unread until I've done them, and then archiving and filing them in different ways so I can refer back as I need to.

As our business has grown and there's just been so many things to keep track of, really being on top of delegating has also been huge for me to be able to stay focused on what I need to do and not getting pulled in a million different directions, or doing things that other people can and should be doing. A big focus of mine in the last few years is trying to almost immediately pass off as much as possible to other appropriate parties, whether that be my social media person or my office manager or my company director. That's how I stay focused and organized as best I can.

YOU HAVE IMPLEMENTED TOOLS AND SYSTEMS TO HELP STREAMLINE TEAM COMMUNICATION. WHAT WORKS BEST FOR YOU, AND WHY?

Chris: I get overwhelmed very easily. I can easily feel like I have too much to do that I just shut down and I don't get anything done. So since we've started moving to Asana in the studio, I have tried to move my entire to-do list into Asana because I like that I can reorder my personal list and then hide away anything that's not of immediate concern.

That's what helps me be productive – being able to go through and say, these are the things I have to get done today, and the rest of it is just going to get folded up where I don't have to look at it all the time and don't have to think about it.

It helps us get done the things that have to get done today while still having a place to keep all of the tasks that need to get done tomorrow or the next day or next week.

Since implementing Asana fewer things are falling through the cracks. It's definitely helped to make sure that those recurring tasks that need to happen every month are happening, and everything is prioritized and delegated efficiently and transparently.

IS THERE ANYTHING THAT YOU WOULD GO BACK AND CHANGE IF YOU WERE GIVEN THE CHANCE?

Kendra: The biggest thing that I wish I had done sooner is getting more confident and clear about my 'why', our studio values, and defining our culture. We always had a mission statement and it was important to me, but I didn't do enough referring back to it when I was making decisions or really instilling it in all of my staff and students and families.

That's been one of the biggest aids to me in the last couple of years in being more confident with every decision that I make, even the unpleasant ones. When you know it's easier to have the hard conversations or make the tough decisions when you have something so concrete and that you really feel passionate about backing it up. I would have made my life a lot easier in some ways and maybe gotten to the cultural place where we are as a studio right now that I'm very happy with and very proud of, maybe gotten there sooner. That's been huge for me.

Planning for growth would have been really helpful. I never had intended to stay a one woman operation. I always dreamt big and had plans to be a business with employees, but I didn't really have a good sense of scale. It was very hard for me to envision anything to this scale so there was too much in my head for too long. If I had been able to think more in advance and what it was going to look like in the future, it would have systematized and put a lot more down on paper.

I anticipated that I wanted to grow, and I planned to grow. It wasn't like I didn't envision myself with this many employees. I envision myself with a lot of employees. I just didn't have the logistics from a systematization standpoint until I was in the midst of it and that it was very hard to backtrack.

HOW DOES YOUR STUDIO STAND OUT FROM OTHER STUDIOS IN YOUR AREA?

Kendra: We are one of the very few studios in our area that does a great job of striking the middle ground. Our studio is right outside of Washington DC and so there are a ton of very serious studios, whether that be elite studios or pre-professional ballet programs. There are also a couple that may not be competitive nor pre-professional ballet, but that are very serious with huge scale, like musical theater productions. Those kinds of studios really require a huge investment of time and money and talent. There's often an audition requirement or even if there's not formally an audition requirement, dancers without a certain level of talent get pushed down in the levels and don't progress through, and don't end up being happy there.

At the other end of the spectrum, there are a lot of community programs that run through the community centers; the county programs, the schools with the public schools; that are extremely recreational. They are running an eight week session and it's very recreational.

We really strike that middle ground where all of our teachers are certified or have degrees, and have great experience. We have a set curriculum and are building lessons upon lessons and year upon year you're progressing through. Our dancers are getting a very high quality dance education, but there's still a place for you if you only want to dance one or two hours a week. If your leg doesn't go behind your head, that's okay. You can still be a huge part of our program.

There are a few other studios that purport to offer that in our area but what we've found is that people aren't comfortable because there's a lot of turnover in their staff. They are not actually devoting a lot of their energy and their focus and quality into their recreational programs. Or they have those programs, but they aren't integrated into the culture of the studio because all their focus goes towards their competitive children or their pre-professional dancers.

We seem to have really found a niche for ourselves in this area where we're really the go-to studio for a pretty large geographic area if you want that middle ground. It's hard to offer a competitive program and offer a recreational program and keep both sides of those happy and integrated into your studio culture and that's something we are really proud of.

WHAT INSIGHTS FROM NON-DANCE INDUSTRIES HAVE YOU BEEN ABLE TO BRING TO THE STUDIO AS A DANCE-HUSBAND?

Chris: Definitely a technological awareness. Early on we were one of the first dance studios that offered online registration before anybody else was offering online registration. We are on top of our email marketing back when lots of dance studios were still mailing out postcards and relying on paper flyers and newspapers.

The bar is rising for all small businesses as far as being where customers are in a way that's not intrusive but is there to make yourself known. There are all of these areas that you've either got to figure it out on your own to be able to work through it, or find somebody who you can trust and pay the premium to handle it. Being confident and competent in the tech-space is only getting more crucial for dance studios so having that awareness and knowing what kinds of questions to ask is very valuable.

It's an ongoing struggle because it may not come as naturally to our staff or to Kendra as it is to me, but it's all so very necessary as we continue to grow. Having expertise coming from that external industry has been huge.

WHAT LESSONS ARE YOU MOST PASSIONATE ABOUT INSTILLING IN YOUR DANCERS?

Kendra: The biggest things that I try to instill in our dancers all comes back to our core studio values. For example, we work a lot on inclusivity, constant self improvement, and positivity. Positivity is something that we focus on a lot across the board. All of our teachers really try to think about body positivity with all of our children.

WHO HAS HAD THE BIGGEST INFLUENCE/S ON YOU AS A DANCE STUDIO CEO?

Kendra: One of the biggest people who influenced me in my ability to start this studio from a business perspective would be my mom. She supports our studio and was a huge help in my initial advertising efforts, and my parents actually co-signed the lease on our first studio space because Chris and I were just married, and had very few assets of our own, so that vote of confidence in me and my idea and my business just meant the world both emotionally and from a logistical perspective. I don't know how it would have happened without them.

From a teaching perspective I had a lot of great college professors that impacted me hugely in the way I teach technically and the way that I interact and relate to my students. The most influential one would be Bill Thomas. He taught a couple of different ballet classes and a couple of modern dance classes that I took in college and he was able to challenge his students and really call them out when they weren't doing enough in some way, shape or form.

He really challenged us, but also really encouraged and built us up. He had a way of celebrating with you when you achieved something. He just struck that balance in a really meaningful way to me. And so that's what I try to model my teaching after.

WHAT ADVICE WOULD YOU GIVE TO AN ASPIRING DANCE STUDIO OWNER?

Kendra: Definitely that it's easier to systemize and organize and get everything laid out earlier – even if you don't think you need it – it's easier to do it now than to do it later. You can always tweak it and grow but to have a good, solid foundation laid out from the systems and organizational administrative processes is really important.

Also to be clear on your vision and using it to make decisions. Customers will challenge you, especially when you're a new business, especially if you're younger than they are. Every time we stood our ground and made the hard choice, we gained more respect from that parent and from every other parent that saw it happen. It made things that much easier next time around. I don't think we've ever regretted standing our ground on our policies, especially when those policies came out of our core values.

It's also crucial to remember that you can go too far with that and be not open to feedback. Sometimes you need to adapt with the market, but if you like your policy and you think it comes from a really good place, you've got to stand behind it and the parents will respect you for it.

Every time I have to disappoint someone or say no, I can do it from a place of compassion and knowing that what I'm doing is the best thing for the studio as a whole.

DANCE STUDIO SECRETS BONUS –
FIND OUT HOW KENDRA AND CHRIS FINALLY ACHIEVED MORE BALANCE IN THEIR LIVES IN OUR EXCLUSIVE BONUS INTERVIEW
DSOA.COM/KENDRA

I have so much admiration for this next studio owner who has been able to scale and grow her studio rapidly without losing the personal touch with her loyal dance families. Not only have Kaitlin's student numbers soared over the last five years in business, but she has been able to do so without compromising the strong quality of training in her studio.

Kaitlin Hague is the CEO of Bayside Dance in Queensland, Australia.

She began her dance studio in 2014 after a portfolio career in the creative industries spanning performing, dance teaching, adjudicating, choreographing and education program management in some of South East Queensland's major performing arts venues.

Kaitlin has a Bachelor of Creative Industries in Dance (Distinction) and in 2017 completed a Master of Arts (Research) investigating talent identification and development in ballet. Her work has been regularly published in *Dancetrain* magazine.

Kaitlin started Bayside Dance in a small hall with seven students. She now employees 17 staff and has 600 students attending class every week, ranging from ages two to adult. She's a bit of a local celebrity, and can't do the groceries without bumping into at least one dance family.

Kaitlin is married to Ivan and has one human baby (Emilia) and two fur babies (Bonnie and Daisy). When she's not at the studio she's out walking along the Wynnum Esplanade, shopping or enjoying a glass of wine and a big bowl of pasta.

Check out Kaitlin's latest studio news at baysidedance.com.au

Chapter Fifteen

SCALING YOUR STUDIO FOR SUCCESS: KAITLIN HAGUE

Bayside Dance

CAN YOU SHARE WITH US YOUR BACKGROUND OUTSIDE OF THE STUDIO, AND HOW IT HELPED YOU GET TO WHERE YOU ARE TODAY?

I started dancing when I was three – my first ever concert dance was the chicken dance and from there I was just in love. I was a 'ballet head' for a little while before getting into jazz, tap and everything on offer. By the time I was about eight or nine, I was doing every style I could.

I was a pretty good dancer, getting distinctions in my ballet exams and I always came to class to work hard and try and get in the front line which of course is the number one goal when you're little and dancing. When I was 12, the studio I danced at closed and so we moved to another local studio and I stayed there all the way through high school.

I applied for Queensland University of Technology (QUT) in grade 12 and was accepted. I went to QUT to do a Bachelor of Creative Industries/Bachelor of Teaching. Because I was at university and there are all these amazing creative things that were opening up, the whole idea of becoming a choreographer, or an independent artist was so tantalizing and amazing. I was seeing all this great work and just being exposed to so much more dance than ever before. I realized, *Actually I*

*want to go and try and make it doing something else first, and if I need
to come back and do my education then I can do it later.* But I never did.

I dropped the education side of my degree – probably to my
parents' distress – but I did really well at university, I graduated with
distinction. Then straight after university I got a paid gig touring
around Queensland dancing in a show where we would perform 12
shows a week. I did that for a year and it was awesome. But I realized
that I didn't like performing as much as I thought I would. As a child in
that environment, you're performing different dances all the time, and
learning new things all the time, whereas doing the same show 12 times
a week was not what I had thought it was going to be.

When I came back from one of our tours, I saw an advertisement for
an admin job at *Dancetrain* magazine and thought, *Oh, I can do that!*

I ended up working for them and worked for them for five years and
that gave me a really great insight into the industry from a different
perspective. I would look after the website or I would look after their
Facebook, and I was doing all sorts of small business management stuff
and saw first-hand how you could be really impactful with a small and
dedicated team.

I loved it. And I got to write as well, which I never thought I would
get to do. I was really excited to have been able to write and I got to
interview amazing people like Sean Parker and Natalie Weir, I got to
interview Li Cunxini, it was amazing.

AT WHAT POINT DID YOU REALIZE THAT YOU WANTED TO TAKE YOUR INDUSTRY EXPERTISE AND OPEN UP BAYSIDE DANCE?

The whole time throughout university and my other jobs, I was still
teaching dance. At one point I was teaching at six different dance
studios, and I was teaching in schools as well. Then I ended up with a
stress fracture in my foot, and I quickly realized that I don't know if I
can keep teaching like this because I was teaching six days a week.

I was working too hard, I had no money, I thought, *I don't know if
I can keep living my life like this.* And I'd been at *Dancetrain* for a long
time and while I loved it, I'd been working from home pretty much for
two years or three years, so I was ready to work alongside people again.

After that, a lot of things happened all at once. My father-in-law had a stroke, and so we moved in with him. About a month later, one of the local dance studios that was really popular shut down suddenly. I had a lot of family friends asking me, "What should I do, where should I take my child?"

I talked about it with my husband and we just decided, let's start small and find a local hall that is free on a Saturday morning, and just start classes and see what happens.

On my first day I had seven children, and a month later I had a website and the business name and all the rest of it. I never think about things for a very long time. I like to move quickly.

Within a couple of weeks, everything was ready to go and by the end of that year we had 55 dancers in a tiny little concert that went for 30 minutes. I knew that if I could do that in six months, I could make this a success.

I did a really big marketing campaign to launch the school properly the following year and that was with classes six days a week. It went crazy and I had over one hundred new students that January.

That was in 2014, and this year in 2019 we have just passed 600 students.

WHAT ARE THE CORE VALUES IN YOUR DANCE STUDIO, AND HOW DO YOU COMMUNICATE THESE WITH YOUR TEAM AND CUSTOMERS?

Dance is so much more than pointing your toes, and that by engaging in dance in a positive and nurturing way, we're building beautiful human beings, not just beautiful dancers. There's so much more to be learned from it than the technical aspects, it develops resilience, it develops creativity, it enhances intelligence, it develops teamwork.

My best friends are dancers that I knew from other little projects I've done here and there along the way. It creates such an unbelievable bond between people, it's fabulous.

Dance is so much more than just dance really, so our values are all about that.

Our values here are, positivity, community, service, respect and safety. We've just added 'quality' as well, which encompasses the quality of teaching, quality of costumes/uniforms, and quality of movement.

Our value of 'service' for example, is reflected in the fact that we get back to people within 24 hours. Our incident reports are filled out on the day and checked off with parents and sent to me and checked in the next day. With the software that we use, we have multiple check-in points if people miss classes so we can check in with them and make sure they are okay.

If someone from our team makes a mistake we always address it and communicate honestly. It's reflected a lot through the way that we run this school. It was really easy when it was just me because I knew that everyone was getting high quality service, but when you add more team members, there is a lot of follow through and a lot of explaining why each touchpoint is important so that the level and quality of service is consistent.

We talk constantly about keeping our competition team environment positive too. Before and after competitions, we might send an email just to remind our parents and dancers, "If you don't have anything nice to say, don't say it at all."

We talk to the children about body language, reminding them not to cross their arms while sitting watching another schools routine, because it doesn't look like they are enjoying it. We then follow up afterwards and say, "Okay, we might not have done as well as we thought this time around, but that was the adjudicator's opinion and our team is so proud of the dancers both on and off stage. Thanks for your continued support of our positive environment."

We're telling them to be positive and then thanking them for being positive afterward. There's a lot about language that we use in our communications that is focused to our value.

WHO ARE YOUR BIGGEST ROLE MODELS?

A couple of years ago I completed my Masters degree, and my supervisor for that is a brilliant lady named Professor Gene Moyle who is also the executive chair of Ausdance National. Gene is a huge inspiration of mine. She was a ballerina who became a performance psychologist working with the Australian Institute of Sport, and has since been published in dozens of reputable essays and publications.

She is a real inspiration of mine because she gets stuff done and was such a smart and clever mentor to me throughout my masters. I also get so much inspiration out of the Dance Studio Owners Inner Circle and our experienced coaches who are amazing.

I also have lots of my friends – the dance teachers or dance studio owners – who I can draw from such a pool of knowledge all the time, which is great. And even sometimes there are dance studio owners who I don't even know in person but have connected with on Facebook and just make me think, *Wow, you're amazing. I'm going to do what you do.*

WHAT ARE SOME OF THE MOST SIGNIFICANT INDUSTRY SHIFTS YOU HAVE SEEN THROUGHOUT YOUR CAREER?

Because I have such a broad knowledge base of work prior to opening the school, I always knew that you couldn't just be a good dance teacher, you had to be good at other stuff (like admin, marketing, planning), or pay people who are good at that to do it for you.

When I started this school I was doing everything myself. I taught everything, I did all my own admin, I did all my own bookkeeping. I did absolutely everything. It was all me. And then slowly you can get other people to come on board.

You have to be a really good communicator, you have to be so much more organized than dance. We find people want information right now, so you've got to be so on top of everything so that you can really manage those expectations. Because people are so busy – they might have dance on Monday, swimming on Tuesday, soccer on Wednesday, rugby on Thursday and then performance team on Friday, then Saturday they are at 17 different birthday parties. Parents are so busy and the demands are really intense and so we need to be so organized.

It's May and I'm already starting to look at next year's schedule for January, because accounting for our growth has to happen so far in advance. Particularly because we are still growing – our oldest children are only 15, so we've got to keep making more classes till they get to 18.

In some ways, technology has made things easier, like having studio software is revolutionary. There's no way I could have this many students and not have studio software.

IN WHAT WAYS HAVE YOU SEEN OTHER STUDIO OWNERS STRUGGLING WITH THEIR GROWTH, AND WHAT WOULD YOUR ADVICE TO THEM BE?

We do too much ourselves, and a lot of us would be 'control freaks' which I pretty much used to be.

It's understandable, for a lot of us handing over things can be really challenging because we want things done a certain way, and a lot of us will have in our head, *Oh, it's going to take me three weeks to train up this person to be able to do this the same way, I would rather now just do it.*

Thinking long term is really challenging. A danger that lots of people run into is trying to do everything all on their own.

It might mean that in some ways their business is profitable, but it's not going to grow, because you're spending so much time working IN the business, you're not working ON it, you're not looking at two and three year projections. You're not spending the time doing the things you really love because you're spending time answering a hundred emails every night before you go to bed.

A lot of studio owners also get very negative sometimes when dealing with customers. Because we know that they haven't read their emails, or they didn't read the newsletter. Having a separation between me and some of the day-to-day emails has been so helpful because I've got someone who's designated job is to get back to the question that if I'm answering it for the 700th time I might find really irritating. It's their job to answer that question politely. We've taken out any emotion or frustration, which has been really helpful.

WHAT'S THE BEST BUSINESS ADVICE YOU'VE EVER RECEIVED?

Systemizing everything creates so much freedom. Having that has been a huge asset to our business. Sometimes we have relief teachers come in and the handover is so simple. I can say, "You've got an iPad with the roll, the music and the curriculum on it. The class starts on time. It finishes on time. Here's incident reports if something goes wrong and XYZ."

So we're certainly systematic in how we set things up, which has been a game changer for me to make sure that we had processes in place.

WHAT'S CHANGED FOR YOU IN YOUR BUSINESS WHEN YOU HAD YOUR DAUGHTER?

So much. My attitude changed in that my studio was no longer the most important thing in my life. My husband will agree, the business seemed more important than him at times, and while in some ways he sees the benefit from what our studio has been able to provide for our families, it's something he has had to deal with.

I ended up going into parenthood really well-prepared because I had lots of advice and lots of mentors who were studio owners that had children.

I knew that I didn't want to be held hostage to my studio when I wanted to be with my child. And vice versa, because I realized that I actually do really love working and that's a huge part of who I am. I love working, I love being intellectually challenged. I adore my studio family. They are wonderful people and it's a really happy place for me to be.

When I wasn't here a lot I did really miss it. When Emilia was first born, I went through that phase of wishing I had a 'normal job' where I don't have to talk to anyone else and can just be a mom for 16 weeks of government maternity leave.

If I need time off or if I need time with Emilia I set a lot of boundaries around my time. And having lots of people at the studio to help with, that has been the key really.

Nobody at the studio has my phone number other than my staff. Out of 400 of parents, I've got two that are my friends on Facebook. I'm very protective of my personal life. I don't answer emails on Sunday. I very rarely work on a Sunday unless it's a recital or a scheduled rehearsal. Or if I'm getting a really big urge to do some work and Emilia's having a really long sleep, but it's my choice – it's not that I have to do it.

I didn't do that early enough to be honest, because even when I was in hospital I was getting a couple of texts and I got my husband to just tell them, "You can figure it out, you know what to do."

WHAT ADVICE WOULD YOU GIVE TO STUDIO OWNERS WHO ARE IN THEIR FIRST FEW YEARS OF OPERATING?

It's a marathon, not a sprint. I've been thinking about this a lot lately. I love things to happen quickly and when it was just me, I could make things happen very quickly. But now that I have a bit of a bigger team, and the studio is growing, things do have to happen a bit more slowly. There's a rollout procedure and to change procedures takes awhile, and to get everybody on board takes a while.

The other piece of advice I would share is that when people show you their true colors, believe them the first time. Whether it's a staff member or a client, if it's not the right cultural or value-based fit for your business, you can't waste time trying to accommodate them.

DANCE STUDIO SECRETS BONUS –
GET A SNEAK PEEK INTO KAITLIN'S STAFF PLAYBOOK IN OUR
EXCLUSIVE BONUS INTERVIEW
DSOA.COM/KAITLIN

Like many of the Studio Owners you have read about in this book, my next guest is one of the founding members of the Dance Studio Owners Inner Circle. Shawna is such a genuine and honest asset to our industry, and I have found a lot of joy in watching her growth over the last five years. Shawna truly has transformed from a studio owner to the CEO of her business.

Shawna Kwan the CEO of Elan Dance Arts in Ontario, Canada.

She's known for her passion, positivity and drive to mentor and impact everyone around her and has been teaching dance for over 20 years across Canada and the U.S.

She has successfully built, and is known for her boys program with over 60 boys currently training at EDA.

Shawna has enjoyed being both the choreographer and a dancer for the feature performance group for the Stihl Timbersports Canadian Championship. She was also, for four years, the creative director for the London Lightning Basketball Team, a three-time championship team from the National Basketball League (NBL). Over the years Shawna has also had the pleasure of working with artists such as Andre 300, 50 Cent and Mark Wahlberg.

Shawna is a loving mom of two beautiful, young, energetic girls. She's always doing what she can to work with and help others. She's often told that her energy is contagious and wants to share that and build that up in as many people as she can!

Check out Shawna's latest studio news at elandancearts.ca

Chapter Sixteen

COMMUNITY OVER COMPETITION: SHAWNA KWAN

Elan Dance Arts

WHAT IS YOUR FIRST MEMORY OF DANCE AS A CHILD?

I actually started dance really late. I started dance class when I was 12 in Ottawa, the capital of Canada, before I moved to London, Ontario to study kinesiology at university. I took a hip hop class there, which didn't exist at the studios when I was dancing, and I happened to be really good at it. They asked me to fill in for the assistant one day, and my teaching blossomed from there. When the hip hop teacher was unable to work because of an injury, they asked me if I could be the teacher.

The program grew so much that they asked if I was interested in directing the whole program. So, I ran the dance program at the university for about six years in total before I thought, *I'm going to open up my own studio.* And that's how that happened. I'd been teaching since I was 17, but the thought of opening a studio had never really occurred to me and now we're just finishing up our 12th year as a studio.

WHAT TOOK YOU BY SURPRISE IN YOUR FIRST THREE YEARS OF RUNNING YOUR OWN BUSINESS?

I don't really remember my first year – it was that intense! I do recall that the majority of people had no idea what I was talking about. We forget that as dance teachers we have our own language, so it was a huge reminder to me that I had to explain everything.

I didn't involve myself in anything to do with the business side of things those first few years. My ex-husband did all of that. He ran everything having to do with business and numbers, and I was the face of the business. The main reason I joined the Dance Studio Owners Inner Circle was because my marriage split and I needed to learn to do everything myself. I never touched anything business related until about four years ago.

TELL US ABOUT SOME OF THE FAILURES YOU'VE EXPERIENCED, AND THE LESSONS YOU'VE BEEN ABLE TO TAKE AWAY FROM THOSE FAILURES.

The thing that I've struggled with the most has been leadership and mentoring with staff because we all underestimate the amount of work and training that we need to do in order to be really effective in that area. I look back at some of my staff that I very much valued and I didn't know how to show them that value. I'm much better at that now, and I would've kept some of them for longer had I just had more experience in that area.

WHAT PROJECTS ARE YOU MOST EXCITED ABOUT RIGHT NOW, AND WHY?

We just launched a brand new preschool program, and we restructured the entire program and registration. That's the biggest project where classes have a new name and a new schedule because until now, we've never had one class per age group. It's always been students at the preschool age could be in the same class for two or three years.

The idea of having them move to a different class each year gives them that sense of accomplishment and that they are moving on and moving up. We've also changed all of our classes to combo classes where they have multiple disciplines, which we didn't do before. We had preschool classes, but each class was a singular discipline. It's clear that the combo class is a trend amongst studio owners who have really successful preschool programs so I'm excited about that.

The big thing that's going to really help the program grow is that I have hired a dedicated preschool director, someone who is running the show and that every parent can communicate with. We also switched everything to three eight-week sessions, which we've never done. It's been a full year. I have a ton of interest, so it's been awesome.

Another thing that I've been working on for a couple of years is a Studio Connect project that I built with my staff. It's a way to connect studios, not only within my city but within other cities and other countries around the world.

One studio picks a song and a studio does a section of choreography before sending that video to another studio to do the next section. Different studios will do different styles, but we're essentially all passionate about the same thing and it's a really cool way to connect us all.

It started out with wanting to get rid of tension between the studios here in my city, but then I connected with so many other studios in Canada and beyond. It's really fun and fulfilling and a way to connect with other studios and help support everybody.

WHY DO YOU THINK YOU HAVE BEEN SUCCESSFUL IN A NICHE WHERE OTHER STUDIOS HAVE FAILED?

I've always had a really successful adult program. I didn't plan on it on purpose, it just happened organically. I had a good group of adults and it really boils down to the community that we create. Adults in particular want to be a part of a community and they want to feel like they are a part of something. So, they want to come to class and if they don't come to class, then they are missed. They participate in the recital and they just have a really great time with each other and it's fun. They are choosing to be there.

My fitness program involves the same thing – that community where they'll post online that they are feeling lazy and that they don't really want to come to class and they need some help. Then all the ladies pipe in, and they are full of encouragement, "Get your shoes on, see you in five minutes!" And they show up. It's just that culture and that community that we've been really successful at creating. They keep coming which allows me to constantly add new people whenever they are ready because I'm always going to have a really great core group of adults there.

ARE THERE ANY OTHER PROFESSIONS THAT YOU WOULD LIKE TO ATTEMPT, AND WHY?

I know that a lot of studio owners struggle with this, but I really like sales, and I would potentially do something in sales. People seem to say that they really like my energy when I'm speaking to them and I don't think that my sales come off as 'salesy'.

We're always having a genuine conversation. For example, there may be a mom registering her daughter for acro, and I'll have a natural conversation that looks something like this:

ME: "It's worth mentioning that if you're open to it, I would recommend a second class for your daughter because it'll really boost her technique and she has already progressed so quickly."

MOM: "Oh, what should she take?"

ME: "Well, ballet ideally, but if ballet isn't her thing, then I would put her in jazz."

MOM: "Thank you so much. I hadn't even thought of that!"

I'm just comfortable chatting with people. I don't shy away from a cross-sell or an upsell and I genuinely appreciate that they want my opinion, and they'll do whatever they want with the information. I very quickly got over feeling upset if I didn't enroll a customer.

It's like dating. Some people are simply not the right fit for you, and the sooner you find that out, the sooner you can focus on the people that may be the right fit for you. If I'm trying to enroll you and you're not interested, and you're not the right fit, it's a waste of both of our times.

WHAT DO YOU LOOK FOR WHEN YOU ARE HIRING A NEW TEACHER?

My expectations are that my teachers are going to work really hard. If they are not meeting my expectations, then I'm going to make sure that I let them know so we can work on it together and not lose any time.

I also always tell my staff that they need to, very early on, explain who they are to the children and why they do what they do. We all teach and communicate in different ways, so it's really important to start off by explaining who you are and why you're there, for example, "Miss Shawna hired me to teach this class because of the XYZ experience" or "The goal that we have for your class is XYZ."

It's really important to remind them why they are in the teaching position that they are in and what the expectations are.

Energy is another big thing, and one of my mentors growing up as a teacher used to always say that from the second that students walk through the door, whatever energy they see in you is the energy that you've set for the class. So, if you're sitting on the ground and you're staring at your phone or you're just talking, or you're yawning, you have now set that energy at a four out of ten for the class. Don't anticipate that your students are going to give you the eight or nine out of ten, because you're giving them a four.

It doesn't matter if you're in the fourth or fifth hour of the night. The people at nine pm should be getting the same energy that you gave at four pm. That's a big thing that I tell my staff, and I find that just greeting your students in a positive way gets around any of that. They need to get used to opening that door for them and welcoming everyone and then you're setting the tone right then and there.

We're also big on our team dynamic with each other. I usually hire like-minded people and we make a really big effort to get them all vibing together. They have to be willing to help each other out and work with each other – which is a big priority for me. There are a lot of staff who seem fine with being on their own and that may work in some studio environments, but in mine it definitely doesn't.

WHAT HAVE BEEN SOME OF YOUR BIGGEST 'HIGHS' AS A DANCE STUDIO OWNER?

After joining the Dance Studio Owners Inner Circle in my third year, we had our first profitable year since I took over. The business was in trouble, and I didn't even know it because I didn't think it was important to know or check in on anything my partner was doing. I thought everything was fine and I had no clue until I went in and started working on it myself. It was really empowering and wonderful to create enough change on my own to have profit

WHAT IMPACT HAS YOUR BACKGROUND IN KINESIOLOGY MEANT TO YOUR STUDIO AND YOUR REPUTATION?

Kinesiology essentially is the study of the body in motion. I did a lot of work on athletic injuries and sports psychology and found it really appropriate to what I was interested in. I was a competitive athlete before I started dance, so I've always been very active. When I started it, I wanted to be a physiotherapist for professional athletes. Further down into my training and closer to when I was graduating I became interested in working with professional dancers as well. I realized that the majority of the patients that I would be working with weren't going to be taking great care of their bodies and that concerned me.

It has put me in a position where I have a lot of knowledge about injuries. My dancers don't fake injuries. They just know that they can't. It helps me hire staff who have really great knowledge of musculoskeletal structures. I like them to explain to the children exactly what they are doing and what parts of the body that they are using and why. The parents and students very much look to me for advice on different kinds of pains. I have a physiotherapist that I've used for all of my injuries and I send all my dancers to her and she can genuinely tell me in detail what is wrong with the students.

I can get them back into dancing and training maybe at a better pace or at a different pace than other people and it helps their rehab in general.

Everything in our bodies is there for a certain purpose. When you injure or strain one thing, you are then putting into action so many things in the body that are there to specifically protect that injury. So, you have to then further protect those other structures.

WHAT IS YOUR FAVORITE RETENTION STRATEGY?
We have dance boxes for our new students, so every new student gets to choose whether they want a classical box or urban box. And that's new this year and they've just absolutely loved that. Other students can buy boxes if they like, but new students get to choose between these boxes. The classical box has a tutu and a hair bow and a hair extension and bubbles. And then, the urban box has a shoe bag and sunglasses, LED shoelaces and a running shoe keychain. It's such a simple welcome gift that elevates their customer experience, and they really enjoy it.

I use the Inner Circle on-boarding system where I do video and audio messages, and we call them personally on the phone in their third week. It makes them feel special and we love to help our dancers feel welcome regardless of when they start. They feel like they are being reached out to and that they are part of something. Again, they just want to be a part of something and they want to feel important and know that you care about them.

WHAT ARE YOUR TOP THREE STRATEGIES FOR ATTRACTING BOY DANCERS TO THE STUDIO AND KEEPING THEM THERE?
We have just over 60 boys at the studio this year and firstly, I have always charged full price for boys. I'm the only studio in my city (out of about 20 studios) who charges full price, and I've always had more boys than anywhere else. I have always had very strong male instructors for my boy classes, and any boys that come to the studio have the option of doing an all boys class or a co-ed class. It's their choice, and I've always had really strong hip hop and break programs.

Retention is the big thing with boys. The more you can get in there, the more that are going to come. I don't really target ads necessarily to boys, but it's really now attributed to our reputation. As soon as you have that strong male instructor in there, it makes it cool to dance. Then, when the teacher says, "Hey, you know what – you're doing really great in hip hop, I think you'd be a really fantastic B-boy, we'd like you to try the break class..." then they normally do it because they look up to these teachers so much.

Finally, offering variety is really huge. Giving them a competitive offer is great because boys stand out at competitions and often do well because they are boys, and they stand out. It makes them feel really special, it makes them want to do more, and it makes them want to be better. We also do awards for our boys, like star B-boy or a hip hop star or most potential male dancer. That's always a coveted thing for the guys.

It's my pleasure to bring you into the world of a Dance Studio Owner who runs her studio every single day based on her core values. Every decision that Lynn makes is aligned with her core values. Over the last three years working together I've been so proud to witness her transformation into a studio owner that prioritizes self care first. It's a rare and wonderful thing to see a Studio CEO ensuring that she is at her best so that she can bring the best to her students and staff.

Lynn Hadden-Quinn is the director and owner of LHQ Danceforce & Wellness Studio in Massachusetts, USA.

She is known for motivating and pushing students to find their love of dance as well as finding the drive within to set goals and achieve their fullest potential in dance, health and life. As a leader she is always on the cutting-edge of the latest trends and technology leading her staff to elevate themselves and their students to strive for greatness inside and outside the classroom.

Lynn has been featured in the *Dance Studio Life* magazine Teacher Spotlight. She also is a certified lifestyle coach and has a passion for wellness and giving back the gift of wellness in her programs at LHQ Danceforce.

She is married and just celebrated her 20 year anniversary. Lynn lives with her husband and son and two dogs. She enjoys Bikram yoga and CrossFit, loves to read, spend time with family and listen to podcasts that keep her cup full.

Check out Lynn's latest studio news at lhqdanceforce.com

Chapter Seventeen

THE VALUES-BASED DANCE STUDIO: LYNN HADDEN-QUINN

LHQ Danceforce & Wellness Studio

TELL US ABOUT YOUR OWN EXPERIENCE AS A DANCER GROWING UP, AND WHAT LED YOU TO BECOME A DANCE STUDIO OWNER?

Like many studio owners and dance teachers, I started at a very young age. I must have been about three or four years old when I started dancing at our local dance studio, and after that I essentially grew up in my home-based studio.

I was very loyal to my studio, which is very different to some of the behaviors and attitudes of dancers these days. I was there with her since I was little and I grew up in the dance studio where the studio owner really mentored me. I was teaching classes at the age of 16 or 17 as an assistant and she was mentoring me into teaching. It was an incredible way to learn the ropes, and I feel like I got a great base in not only teaching, but being able to become a good role model.

Right away I started to see how much I really enjoyed teaching, on top of my love of performing and I just knew at a young age that teaching and mentoring was the direction I wanted to go. Eventually my teacher and I decided to merge and take our efforts into our own studio together when I was 21, with less than 30 students.

HOW HAVE SOME OF YOUR PREVIOUS JOBS IMPACTED ON YOUR BUSINESS DECISIONS IN THE STUDIO?

I worked at our local Six Flags, which was a huge amusement park, and worked in every aspect of that park that you could think of!

After that I worked at a costume company where I was a costume seamstress supervisor for many years, and continued to work there as a second job when I opened the studio. I taught the entire sewing floor how to sew the costumes which was a really valuable lesson in leadership that I continue to draw on to this day.

It was a challenge that I loved, because a lot of the people who I was supervising didn't speak English and there were so many walks of life that I touched and learned a lot about culture and effective systems and communication.

That job has also given me some great skills in costume concepts and those sewing skills that always come in handy at costume time, as well as being very therapeutic for me to actually be able to sit and sew.

YOU RUN A VALUES-BASED BUSINESS – WHAT DOES THIS MEAN TO YOUR STUDIO AND YOUR DANCERS?

This is something that has changed a little bit over the years, because to be honest in those earlier days I didn't go as deep as I do now – it was a much more surface-level driving force. I was young and I just loved to dance and I loved to teach and that was it.

Today it definitely is deeper for me. I do want to make a difference.

I feel like today children need teachers and mentors and leaders who are role models because when you look around at the larger world, sometimes there aren't a lot of positive role models out for our children and teens. I lead by example by making sure that I take care of myself and it's become a huge value and priority to be a good role model for these children. I also make sure that I am always on top of things, and have their best interests at the front of mind which we are also very conscious of making the parents see this too. When I'm making healthy habits in my own life, I can see the actual culture changing in the studio because I'm leading that culture.

I've been in business for a long time, but only more recently have I talked about and taught our core values and really hitting it hard the past two years which came about because I have such a spirit for dance.

It's in our logo, and our tagline so we just had to really work on how we were going to dig deeper into those values to make a bigger impact.

Now, we drill those values into our newsletters, our social media, our marketing, and the language we use in the classroom. We have a 'Dancer Of The Month' which always draws back to one of our core values. One month it's TEAMWORK. The next month it may be PASSION. We pick a dancer during the month who has displayed passion in their training and life, which has just been one example of something that has really brought everything together in terms of our core values.

I never really realized the impact this would have on the studio overall, until I started really digging in and doing it. As far as my culture goes, I know that when I'm leading the culture that it's going in the right direction.

WHO ARE YOUR ROLE MODELS, AND WHY?

First of all I have to say my parents were two of my role models. I was really lucky to grow up under the direction of two hardworking, very dedicated people who pushed through any obstacles in life, and all while having fun. My father always took care of himself and he always had a great time, but he was a hard worker.

Both my father and mom were both very powerful role models.

I also had Carol, teacher and mentor who was just another great human. She modeled wonderful behavior in the way she ran her studio, and also in her personal life. A lot of my own habits and behaviors as a mentor are a credit to her for the way she modeled those to me.

CAN YOU TELL US ABOUT THE IMPACT THAT RUNNING YOUR DANCE STUDIO HAS HAD ON YOUR 20-YEAR MARRIAGE?

Well to start with, I absolutely need to recognize my husband as a tremendous inspiration in all areas of business and life. In a lot of ways it's been a really rough 20 years and we have certainly had our share of ups and downs.

My husband comes from a very tough upbringing – the complete opposite to me. He also runs a business and is just one of those people who gets right to the point and says it just like it is. His influence has always helped me be strong in that way. He has also been through a lot in his life and battled with addiction, but I've also watched him work through any obstacle that he's come up against along the way.

He's now been sober for 14 years, and it's all due to putting in the hard, consistent work on his end. It's an incredibly inspiring thing to witness.

For me, dance has been huge in helping our marriage through the roughest days, weeks and months.

I have to say, if I didn't have my studio, I don't think we would still be married. Along our journey we've had the ups and downs where I've really had to find something to obviously keep me sane, and if I had a 'regular job' I don't know that I could have been as strong as I am today because in the dance class, you have no choice but to be that role model. You have to go in and put your acting face on because those little children don't care about what's behind closed doors.

Drawing on that really helped to keep me in a good space and also gave me the courage to work through the challenges and continue to grow a business.

YOU'VE BEEN IN BUSINESS FOR 26 YEARS NOW – WHAT ARE SOME OF THE BIGGEST CHANGES YOU HAVE SEEN IN THE INDUSTRY DURING THAT TIME?

The most significant shift I have seen is in the time-stress on everybody, and it's not just the children but it's also the parents who are really feeling the time-stress. When I look at the expectations being placed on our children and their parents, there is a huge difference – look at homework, as an example. We never had the homework that these children have, and they have so much more on their plates.

It means that holistically, we have a responsibility now to teach differently. We have to look at things differently.

I also see that dancers today are making more excuses. They are not as focused on the whole, they don't take as much pride in themselves, and a lot of them don't respect adults as much as they used to. Everybody's so focused on everybody else, and really hung up in 'what's the next best thing?'

I never had that carrot dangling in front of me. I had one role model. I had one teacher that I grew up under, and most significantly we didn't have the social media that these children have dangling in front of them.

These days a huge part of our focus as dance educators is getting the children to learn to not make excuses, how to focus, how to take pride and care for themselves, and ultimately how to show respect for the art and their bodies. We are now preparing them for all these other aspects of being great humans, and while I always think this was a part of dance, today it's becoming part of your class plan.

WHAT LESSONS IN BUSINESS HAVE HAD THE BIGGEST IMPACT ON YOUR PERSONAL LIFE?

A huge one for me has been mindfulness. Creating my morning routine, practicing meditation and mindfulness has been just huge for me and I feel like it's balanced me as a person.

I have also learned a lot of things the wrong way, so if I give any advice to people, the first thing will always be 'don't ignore your injuries', and make it a non-negotiable to take care of yourself first. Over the past five years I've really been focused on getting out of pain from an injury I sustained in my twenties, which has consequently filtered into the studio because I'm so passionate about injury prevention.

It's so important to us to make sure that these children are taking care of themselves and making sure that they are doing the right thing by their bodies, and that we as a studio are training these children and making sure that they are not injuring themselves.

This chapter features another inspiring husband and wife team who have taken their studio from strength to strength as they have grown over the last eight years in business. Rebecca and Ryan are fearless when it comes to innovating in their business, and I've always been impressed by their generosity in our community of Dance Studio Owners.

Rebecca and Ryan Bickerton are the owners of Dance Stream Victoria (DSV) in Victoria, Australia.

Having grown up in country Victoria, Rebecca commenced her dance training at the age of five at a local dance school. She completed many exams in classical ballet, jazz and tap which led to her receiving her ATOD Associate Classical Teaching Diploma.

After completing a Bachelor of Arts/ Bachelor of Education degree, Rebecca completed full time dance training at Dance World Studios in 2008.

Rebecca has been teaching dance for 18 years and has choreographed many troupes, solos, duos and trios that have been successful at eisteddfods and competitions around Victoria.

Working behind the scenes, Ryan provides the integral business support to ensure DSV provides the best possible training for all students. While sourcing the latest dance equipment, current industry dance teachers and providing state of the art facilities, Ryan also provides the financial, planning, administrative, studio maintenance, prop building, costume repair and studio support.

Check out Rebecca and Ryan's latest studio news at dancestreamvictoria.com.au

Chapter Eighteen

FINDING YOUR WORK AND FAMILY BALANCE: RYAN & REBECCA BICKERTON

Dance Stream Victoria

YOU BOTH MET THROUGH DANCE – TELL US ABOUT YOUR OWN JOURNEY AS DANCERS AND HOW THAT HAS INFLUENCED HOW YOU RUN YOUR BUSINESS TODAY.

Rebecca: I grew up in a musical family – my mom's a guitar teacher and I have lots of family members who are involved in music. When I was young I always had an interest in that music around me but I started dance just because my best friend was doing dance classes and I wanted to do it too. My friend quit six months later at the age of five, and I kept going forever.

I always had a lot of support in that area, because we all had a high appreciation for the arts. When I was 12 years of age I started choreographing a lot of my own dances and discovered that I really loved that side of things.

Both my parents are school teachers, so although teaching was in the blood I always wanted to open a dance studio. I liked the idea of being able to create something that had my own stamp on it and be able to help children grow into great dancers. I did like the idea of eventually being able to work for myself, but that developed more over time.

I trained as a school teacher, and when I opened the studio I was able to work as a high school teacher for six years until the studio was financially stable enough that I could leave that job.

Ryan: I also danced when I was younger. My sister was dancing and as a surprise to my grandmother, my dad got me into dancing to be in the recital one year. From there on I kept dancing to the point where I got into an elite ballet school. I ended up quitting at the age of 16, and then went in to playing football and archery and naturally wanted to try different things. Years later I met up with Rebecca, and it turned out that we had been competitors back when we were both dancing.

Fast-forward a few years and we are now married with two children and a dance studio!

RYAN, WHAT DID YOU THINK WHEN REBECCA TOLD YOU THAT SHE WANTED TO OPEN A DANCE STUDIO AND EVENTUALLY GIVE UP HER SCHOOL-TEACHING CAREER?

Ryan: After we got married I had started a career in civil engineering and supported Rebecca through a year of full-time dance. She worked a year in retail and then a couple of years teaching at a school before she came to me with the bombshell – she wanted to start a dance studio.

I said no.

Actually, I think I said, "That's the worst thing I can ever think of" because I knew what the good, the bad and the ugly of dance schools looked like. Deep down I knew that it was what she really wanted to do so of course I supported it and wanted to help get the business started on the right foot. We started in a logical way and built from the ground up by hiring local halls.

Rebecca: We literally started from scratch. We were in an area that we'd only moved to recently and had no reputation whatsoever. If we had opened a studio where we both grew up, the dance circles all knew us. We'd both danced there all our lives, and I'd taught there for a number of years. Here on the other hand, we had to gradually build our reputation without the boost of being locally-famous.

WHO DO YOU LOOK UP TO AS A CREATIVE ARTIST AND A BUSINESS OWNER?

Rebecca: I was very close to my private lesson teacher, Judy Fildes who inspired me in lots of elements of running the business as well as the artistry.

She was very selfless with time that she gave to people, and while I've learned that you have to value your own time, I don't think it was a bad thing in terms of the culture of the studio. I started out modeling my own studio around all the positives that she demonstrated.

When I was older, I worked quite closely with her and I had some valuable insights into the background workings of the dance studio. It inspired me both in how I would do certain things the same way, and how I could also do things differently. I came out of that work knowing what I wanted to try and also what I wanted to avoid.

Another wonderful mentor and support for me has been Karen Malek who is Australian dance royalty and also the co-owner of the studio I grew up in. She was strict, but not unreasonable and continues to be a powerful role model. She has been open and generous with support since I opened the studio, and I do believe all studio owners need a mentor like that. Someone they can get on the phone and ask, "What should I do with this?" or "What do you think of that?" or "Have you encountered this before?" She's always been 100% willing to help whenever I've needed it and I'm very grateful for that.

TELL ME ABOUT YOUR DYNAMIC AS A HUSBAND AND WIFE TEAM IN BUSINESS IN YOUR EARLY DAYS?

Ryan: It was very much a good cop, bad cop vibe in the early days when Rebecca was doing so much teaching. It was beneficial to be able to separate the admin and the customer service so that the teaching and the reception weren't overlapping, and there weren't as many blurred lines with parents feeling as though our main teacher was accessible 24/7.

When we had a difficult parent, we knew that our answers would be on the same page and people didn't push my buttons as much compared to when they were dealing with Rebecca. As much as it shouldn't be that way – and it has gotten a lot better – that's just the way it was when she was young and had less experience as the business owner.

As a man in the studio, knowing how a dance school runs and knowing so much about dance not only surprised a lot of our new clients, but it gave me some credibility as well with the dancers.

WHAT ARE SOME LESSONS YOU'VE LEARNED FROM PREVIOUS JOBS THAT HAVE HAD AN IMPACT ON HOW YOU RUN THE STUDIO?

Ryan: My Excel skills and setting up systems and spreadsheets have really changed the game for our business operations. We have connected with other studio owners and seen some of the challenges they have in that area, so having it come as second-nature is huge in both our reporting and forecasting.

There are other elements in Industrial Relations and Human Relations, dealing with customers and difficult people that are helpful as well as being open-minded and aware of changing your communication style based on who you are working with. Combining the two industries for me makes it well-rounded and allows me to cross-over with our systems and industry experience.

Now that we've had children my involvement has shifted to taking on more family responsibilities while Rebecca continues to grow the studio.

WHEN STARTING FROM SCRATCH IN YOUR FIRST YEAR, WHAT STRATEGIES WORKED FOR YOU TO ATTRACT NEW STUDENTS INTO YOUR STUDIO?

Rebecca: We started with a flyer drop which, at the pre-Social Media time, was probably the closest thing we could get to targeted Facebook Ads. We had a clear call-to-action as well as a free class pass offer and it worked great.

Across the entire town with family, we walked everywhere to drop these flyers into mailboxes and we were so happy when 90-100 people registered for a trial class from that. We went from zero to 45 fully registered dancers in one week, and right there it started to feel like a proper business.

It's very interesting how times have changed, from that initial flyer that we did was eight years ago compared with avenues and opportunities to market the business today – I'm not actually sure whether it's become easier, or more challenging to attract new students when looking at marketing strategies because of how rapidly that landscape is evolving.

DANCE STUDIO SECRETS BONUS –
DOWNLOAD OUR FREE STUDIO OWNERS READING LIST AT
DSOA.COM/DSV

This incredible studio owner runs the type of studio that I wish I went to as a child. Darby has a huge heart and the ambition to match it, leading the industry in training and opportunities for her dancers. Her energy is electric, her generosity boundless and I have no doubt that her legacy in this industry will embrace us for years to come.

Darby Iva Pack is the CEO of the Maryland Academy of Dance located in Maryland, USA.

The school was founded in 2011 and to date Ms Darby serves over 300 students.

As a certified teacher with 21 years of teaching under her belt, she has developed into a teaching artist in ballet, modern, African, liturgical dance and composition/choreography. She has had the pleasure of teaching on faculty at Coppin State University, and for Baltimore County public schools and continues to be a teacher, choreographer and mentor to the next generation of dancers around the world. She holds a BFA from Virginia Commonwealth University in Dance Performance/Choreography and has received scholarships to study at the Alvin Ailey American Dance Theater, Bates Dance Festival and American Dance Festival.

Darby is also certified to teach acrobatics and children with special needs. Darby is a mother to one amazing little girl and loves to spend time with family and friends.

Check out Darby's latest studio news at mdacademydance.com

Chapter Nineteen
BUILDING YOUR LOYAL FAN BASE: DARBY PACK

The Maryland Academy Of Dance

WHAT IMPACT HAS YOUR OWN BACKGROUND AS A DANCER HAD ON YOUR VISION FOR THE STUDIO?

I started at what a lot of us in the industry would refer to as a 'Dolly Dinkle School of Dance', where you don't really get any training but you do get a lot of enjoyment. From ages three to 12, I was not training – I was just enjoying movement, and my mom was paying an astronomical amount of money for me to do that. When I went to eighth grade a performing arts school opened, and I was able to study dance during my school days.

That is when I started training for real, and compared with other serious dancers it was a very late start. I understood movement, but I did not understand anything about terminology or technique or how to do a real plié, what a tondu really was, how to spell it, or what it meant.

That eighth grade year, I

learned enough information to look decent at the high school level, and was able to get a seat in the performing arts high school. For those four years, although I really felt like I was playing catch-up, I was still learning enough information to be in the running for college. Then I decided to major in dance in college.

About two years into college at Virginia Commonwealth University, I realized that I wanted to teach, and I no longer had that desire to perform. I had taught at my church's 'Dance Ministry', and I enjoyed that process. I enjoyed working with non-dancers, and enjoyed people learning new information and going through that process.

I ended up completing my degree in dance performance and choreography and when I came home, I worked as a 'regular human' at a title company for a year, and realized that I needed to follow my heart in the process. I wound up working just here and there teaching classes where I could. Apparently I had too much free time, because I had a baby during that time as well!

After the birth of my daughter I began teaching for a university, and that was a stepping stone for developing and learning how to run a program. Later on, I wound up teaching a dance ministry class for the community, and that's where my school originated from. The birth of the school was truly based on the voice of the Lord, and when I heard the calling that, "It's time to open a school" – I went ahead and opened a school.

YOU EXPERIENCED RAPID GROWTH IN YOUR FIRST THREE YEARS – WHAT DID YOU NEED TO CHANGE ONCE YOU MADE THE JUMP FROM A 'HOBBY BUSINESS' TO A 'GO-TO STUDIO'?

In our first year over Summer, we had about ten students and I knew nothing about running a school. I knew how to teach dance classes, I knew how to engage with people, but I did not know a thing about the business aspect of it. I'm glad there were only ten because we definitely were being baptized by fire that first year we were open.

Although we had only ten students, I knew I had to set this business up like I had 100 students so I created a website. I advertised, set up a Facebook page and a business email address so that I had an online presence. A local studio closed, and when those dancers and their parents went online looking for a studio in the area, we were ready for them.

Based on that, my ten students grew to 60, and 60 grew to 150 by our third year. 150 turned to 200 and the numbers just kept growing.

It was in our third or fourth year that I finally realized that I needed help with the system process, because I was at my maximum capacity for what I knew how to do. The accounting got harder, the payroll got harder, class scheduling got harder. It was growing at a pace that I didn't any longer know how to operate it, and I didn't have time for trial and error because every year, every opportunity counts.

That's how I came across Clint's book *Dance Studio Transformation* which was exactly what I needed – a dummy-proof process that was easy to understand and to see what I needed to be doing.

WHAT IS YOUR 'WHY'?

One thing I do believe in is purpose and destiny. As far as my own life is concerned, I do believe that my gift is teaching. I think that dance just happens to be the way that I teach, and the method that I get to teach many different kinds of people. I am so strong in my faith and I do believe that I'm preparing gifts for the Kingdom, but I also want to be sure that my dancers are getting sound training.

My mom spent a lot of money thinking that she was paying for training, but as a child when it was time for me to prove what she had

paid for, there was nothing to show for it. As a result, one thing I'm very clear with my parents and my community is I will always be honest about what I'm offering, and what I'm capable of doing. Every child will be able to take what they learn here, and go into the world of dance and survive in it.

My 'why' is to create an environment where my dancers are really training. And that they have a community, a safe space, a trusted space for the parents and for the child to know that they're growing.

We are what you would call a 'Black studio', with 95% African American, and maybe 5% of mixed race or Caucasian dancers. It is my promise to these dancers and their parents that they can walk into the room no differently to any non-minority dancer out there, and when the parents drop their children off at our school it is an extension of their home. They're going to be well trained, and they're also going to know the etiquette and how they have to act in a certain dance environment.

I'm not expecting my dancers to be the best, but I am expecting them to represent a certain aesthetic and standard of training when they go places. I always tell them, "You may never win the competition, you may never win the golden prize, but if the judges call you out for good behavior, professionalism and etiquette, then we are winners." We can get them there technically one day, but those little things make a big difference.

I believe that I'm preparing these children for their life and how to manage their lives and to be respectful and responsible adults in the world.

HOW HAS YOUR ROLE AS A LEADER EVOLVED OVER THE LAST FIVE YEARS?

My leadership skills have grown immensely, especially my ability to let go of control. In the past two years, my ability to deal with conflict has

been tested. I know that in my first few years, I avoided it at all costs because in my mind, I had to keep everybody happy. As the school grew, I realized that I had to stand firm in what I knew was right, and then those who would stay would stay, and those who would go would just go. It isn't my job to keep people happy, but to create an environment and a service to people.

My mind shifted, especially when joining the Dance Studio Owners Inner Circle, where I discovered that I just had to stand firm on my values, and that those people who were supposed to be part of the journey would be – whether that's the parent, the child, the teacher, or the admin staff.

I don't ever feel like I'm changing my values anymore, but as the school grows I certainly am faced with bigger levels of conflict that continue to test me in my leadership and maintaining that sense of integrity. I've become a better leader over the years, but there's still so many areas that I'm growing in, trying to balance it and still be fair, honest, and maintain the values and integrity of our school.

WHO ARE YOUR BIGGEST ROLE MODELS IN BUSINESS, AND WHY?

My #1 role model would have to be my 'Dance Mom', Stephanie Powell. Stephanie has been 100% influential in me doing it on my own. She owns a studio herself, and her mentorship has meant the world to me over these years. She's extremely honest with me about everything. When I'm right, when I'm wrong, when it's good and it's bad, she's always been there to guide me and give me the right instruction for the moment. Even with the hard conversations, she's always given me a way to approach and still maintain integrity and dignity at the same time.

I went to her summer dance camp as a teenager, and that was the first Black dance experience I had really had. She was the first person who was honest with me about my potential in dance, and about being black in this dance world so that I knew what that expectation looked like. Over the years, we've grown closer and closer. Stephanie and her sister, Yvonne were so helpful in my journey and I've always been able to go to them for the 'how-to's.

Another huge influence in my life and my business is my mom. She has always been a cheerleader, even if she's had doubt in her mind, she's never verbalized it to me. She may ask questions that make me think, but she's never told me no, no matter what it was. Even when I said I was going to major in dance at college. At first, she was thinking in her head, *Absolutely not, I'm not paying for you for the rest of my life. You're going to have to get a real job. This is not going to work.* Then we went to go see Alvin Ailey, and at the end of the show, I cried my eyes out. I must have looked at my mom like, *Didn't you love it?* And she just knew that if it moved me that deeply, that she would have to let go of whatever her idea for me was, and allow me to just follow my heart.

No matter what the outcome would be, she has always allowed me to follow my heart. And for that, I am eternally grateful to her.

On the other hand my dad who I love dearly is a different story. His attitude when I decided to open the dance school would have been *You've lost your damn mind. You need your 401K and your insurance, go back to work!*

He comes from the tradition of working hard and retiring, but to me it always felt like there was a better way for me to be a single parent, and to control my day, and what I do with my time. And it just happened to look like a dance studio.

WHAT IS THE BEST ADVICE YOU COULD GIVE TO ANYONE WHO IS THINKING ABOUT OPENING A STUDIO OF THEIR OWN?

My biggest advice would be to create systems and follow them to the letter. That would be my best advice, is to create a clear plan of action before opening.

When I opened, I shot from the hip with no systems in place, and it cost me time, energy, stress, friendships, and relationships. It cost a lot to not have a clear plan. At that time my concern was to keep everybody happy, because in my mind if they were happy, they would stay.

That attitude cost me a lot, because when I did finally have to create rules and systems, people were resisting it because 'We've been doing it this way for so long.' For that reason, I strongly suggest making a clear guide for how the school should be run before it opens.

In my first year, I was just a dance teacher, not a business owner. But, if I could go back and approach it as a business owner who loves dance, I do believe I would be further along in the process.

The saying goes that great things come in small packages, and from the moment I met this powerhouse I knew that she was the woman behind this proverb. Louise is a dynamo in running a high-calibre program and her ambition knows no boundaries when creating a vision for the future for her studio. I am constantly inspired by her resilience and attitude, and know that you will take so much value from her lessons and experience in this chapter.

Louise Wilkinson is a performing arts studio owner based in Newcastle, Australia.

An accomplished vocalist and dancer, she spent her formative training years under the dance direction of Miss Marie Walton-Mahon, training in all aspects of ballet, modern, contemporary and jazz, before adding singing to her performance repertoire in the late 80s.

Louise has appeared in many performances including big bands, cheer squads, rock outfits and musical theater before commencing her teaching journey in 2000.

Louise has produced and stage managed many key events including entertainment concepts for national sporting teams and major festivals. Louise was entertainment and floor manager for the historic Jets versus LA Galaxy match at a sold out Hunter Stadium, hosting David Beckham.

She has successfully run performing arts schools for the past 19 years. Her passion is fostering young talent and producing industry standard performers.

Standing only five feet tall Louise has an obsession with high heels and has an impressive and eclectic collection. She operates at her best after a vanilla latte most mornings.

Check out Louise's latest studio news at australiandance.com.au

Chapter Twenty

CREATING YOUR LEGACY: LOUISE WILKINSON

Australian Dance And Talent Centre

CAN YOU REMEMBER WHEN YOU FIRST FELL IN LOVE WITH THE PERFORMING ARTS?

My dance journey started when I was three, when my mother was a friend of a very well-known ballet teacher in Australia called Marie Walton-Mahon. We went to her house when I was 18 months old and she watched me walk across the lounge room and she said, "Hang on a second..." I was walking in turnout, so she had a look at my legs and got me to stretch my feet and told my mom, "As soon as she's three years old, you have to send her to me."

I started ballet classes and fell in love with ballet, I absolutely loved it and I was really good at it. I went through all of my Royal Academy of Dance grades up to Intermediate level before starting summer classes at the Australian Ballet School. That's what I thought my journey was going to be – I was going to be a ballerina and that was it.

Fast forward to the day I was doing a duet with my partner, and another dancer came up behind him, tickled him, and I fell. My knee was badly injured and at that elite level there was no getting it back. It was devastating. I'd never done a sport or anything else before because I just danced every spare second I had.

I went back to school and I was quite depressed, when a friend of mine invited me to try The Johnny Young Talent School, which was the first performing arts school of its type in my area. The basic package had jazz (which I had never done) and singing in it. I absolutely loved it and became part of the performance team where I met my singing mentor, Rita Azzopardi who took me under her wing and started developing my singing voice.

I spent some time performing professionally before I fell into teaching at the age of 19, then I got married very young at the age of 22, and continued teaching weekends while working my day job in media at the *Newcastle Herald*.

When I fell pregnant I knew that I didn't want to go back to the Herald, so I put an ad in the newspaper and started teaching singing lessons privately – and from there it blossomed from my passion into my business. At that stage of my life, it was extremely accidental and grew quicker than I could cope with which resulted in a lot of business mistakes because I simply didn't have the right systems in place.

TELL US ABOUT YOUR EXPERIENCE IN TAKING OVER A DANCE STUDIO, RATHER THAN SETTING UP YOUR BUSINESS FROM SCRATCH.

I had a friend who had her studio on the market so we went out for coffee to chat about it. We had two exactly opposite skill sets – she was extremely detail-oriented and into the day-to-day running of the studio, where I was a big-picture thinker who also loved the marketing side of things. I wasn't sure that I was ready to jump into a studio of that size (about 250 students back then) and really doubted whether I knew enough or was confident enough to take things over.

We ended up going into a business partnership in the beginning of 2016 where we grew the student numbers from 250 to 350 over two years.

At the end of 2018 my business partner had graduated from University and had been happily working as a teacher in schools for two years, so we agreed that I would buy her out of the partnership.

We've now grown to the studio's all-time high of 400 students this year, and my ex-business partner and I have maintained a great relationship.

WHAT DRIVES YOU TODAY AS THE CEO OF YOUR STUDIO?

Performing arts is the vehicle for changing lives and building resilient, open-minded children, and these skills that we are teaching them in the classroom drive them in all different areas of their lives. That's what I want to leave behind.

We may not be a school that is turning out students that would go to the Australian Ballet, but certainly we are turning out students that could go and confidently audition for a Broadway show. At its core, what drives me forward is the community that we are building and the lives that we are changing through what we do.

WHO DO YOU LOOK UP TO, AND WHY?

My ballet teacher, Marie Walton-Mahon is still to this day a huge inspiration. She was kind, but strong and the impression that she made on me goes far beyond what she taught me in the classroom.

I love Oprah, because she came from nothing. She was fired from her first job and the amount of lives that she touches and the success that she's had, without stomping on people's heads, is phenomenal. That's such a big part of it for me – I don't believe that you have to be a cold hard woman to be successful. I love her story and I love how much grace and empathy she has for other people, and the fact that she just didn't let anything stop her.

I know this won't resonate with everyone, but I also look up to the Kardashians when it comes to business, and the reason is because they have built an empire through smart business decisions, leveraging their product and finding a way to connect with people. Kylie Jenner has not spent one cent on marketing, ever. That's amazing to me, and it's because one smart woman, Kris Jenner works hard! She has come up with this brand and this identity that has catapulted their success. She has built out the revenue streams in her business in an amazing way. As controversial as they may be, they certainly aren't sitting around doing nothing.

WHAT ARE SOME OF THE BIGGEST CHANGES YOU'VE SEEN IN THE INDUSTRY THROUGHOUT YOUR CAREER, AND HOW DO YOU COMBAT THESE SHIFTS?

The biggest change that I have seen is technology, and it's both our friend and our foe in this industry.

It has heightened awareness of dance in all forms. We can get online and see some amazing talent, whereas the only way you could do that 15 years ago was to go to a live show. I believe that has been beneficial and has brought a lot more exposure, in particular with shows like *American Idol, So You Think You Can Dance* and *America's Got Talent.*

The flip side of that is with the amount of technology that they are using now, dancers don't hold information or have the same work ethic as they did 15 years ago.

We know that learning how to dance or how to sing is a meandering process, but now we have a generation of dancers who expect answers and results in an instant. Because of the amount of time that they scroll through Instagram, Facebook, and watch YouTube clips, the information goes in and it goes out just as quickly because they can't process the amount of information they are getting every day.

It means we've had to change the way that we teach to get them to understand that they are not going to nail a triple pirouette in their first week, because that's what they've seen on Instagram. We've had to change the way that we approach a class, because children used to be happy working towards something and seeing improvement over a long period of time. We've had to approach it as 'edutainment'. We are focusing more on making the class fun and building in the technique so that they retain it, because they are more likely to remember it if they are entertained.

In terms of the opportunities for our dancers, the opportunities are growing because there's more access to open auditions, and agents are more accessible than they used to be. At the end of the day there is more opportunity than there used to be for our performers, but the challenge has been how we get them to a level where they can take advantage of those opportunities.

WHAT 'A-HA' MOMENT OR MOMENTS HAVE SHAPED YOUR APPROACH TO RUNNING YOUR BUSINESS?

In 2016 when I had just taken over the business, I was sitting at my desk making a playlist for a recital when my arm went numb and I didn't feel right. I didn't know what to do, so I rang my dad who said, "Listen, I'm going to call an ambulance and I'll meet you over there."

The paramedics couldn't stabilize my blood pressure, and there was a definite numbness on my left side. I went into the CT machine and the doctors came back and told me that what I was having was called a migraine anomaly. But there had also been an 'incidental finding', where they had discovered a non-ruptured aneurysm in my brain.

It was found by a complete accident. We went through a series of tests to find that the aneurysm was large and it was dangerous. Three months into coming onboard with this business, I had to have brain surgery and in that time I had two weeks to get my life together and my affairs in order in case the outcome wasn't great.

I had to think about my legacy, I had to write my will, I had to write my living will, and I had to write letters to my daughters for their 18th and 21st birthdays. I wrote letters for their weddings and first children, just in case I wasn't there. I went into surgery not knowing whether I would be able to run this business when I got out.

What I realized is that what I wanted more than anything else was for the studio to continue, with or without me. I wanted the lives that I was touching to continue to be touched by performing arts. We are incredibly blessed to be able to be entrusted with their performing arts journey, and what we are building in our business is a legacy that needs to carry on. It's bigger than just us.

In 50 years time, I want this center to be pumping and I want there to be another director sitting in this chair who is as passionate as I am, and that was my big takeaway. We are building a platform that needs to continue long after we're gone.

In this chapter you will meet a Studio Owner who truly embodies what it means to 'dream big'. Shannon possesses a rare and unparalleled ability to tackle a big vision and is both thoughtful and intentional about the way she goes about achieving that goal.

Shannon Westveer is the co-owner of All About Dance in Illinois, USA.

The mission of the studio is to make disciplined dance instruction fun through love, community and creativity. With more than 700 children in regular attendance, each child gets to experience the art of dance, promoting self-confidence, positive values and success.

She has an extensive dance background that includes ballet, jazz, tap and hip hop training. Given her love for performing, Shannon participated in numerous dance competitions and pageants over the years. Shannon has taken this philosophy worldwide in starting an annual dance camp in Lamardelle, Haiti, where for the past three years she along with other teachers, staff and students have spread the love of dance during a weeklong camp for 150 Haitian students.

Through the summer of 2017, Shannon and her husband David have been residing in Chicago, IL. Their family includes their two biological daughter's Addison (age 12) and Audrey (age ten) and their adopted son Lensky (age eight). They are now thoroughly enjoying the next chapter in their lives – playing daily while working remotely and living in Telluride, CO!

Check out Shannon and Jessica's latest studio news at allaboutdance.org

Chapter Twenty-One

A NEXT-LEVEL DANCE STUDIO EXPERIENCE: SHANNON WESTVEER

All About Dance

YOU HAVE QUITE A UNIQUE BACKSTORY, HAVING BOUGHT INTO AN ESTABLISHED STUDIO. CAN YOU TELL US A BIT ABOUT YOUR DANCE STUDIO JOURNEY SO FAR?

I started dancing when I was two-and-a-half. I lived all over the southern part of the US growing up, and had a lot of different dance teachers and different experiences. All of which I loved. I did the whole pageant scene and just really loved being on stage. I danced in college recreationally on dance teams for fun before I went for a degree in marketing and advertising. And then when I transferred out to Northern Arizona University, I was in my last final two years of college, and I was assisting a teacher there for a community center dance program.

I worked with her for two years and then she tragically passed away from cancer so I took over the program during my senior year of college. I had learned so much from her and that's where my first love of teaching really little children came from. Just the joy that they brought into the classroom, and I started thinking, *Wow, I think I can really do this and have an impact and make a difference in these childrens' lives.*

Fast-forward to 2004 and my husband and I were thinking about starting our family all at the same time that I wrote a whole business plan. Ultimately, for his career change, we decided to come back to the midwest to be closer to family and start over, so we moved to Chicago in 2006.

I was at a party one night and met a friend of mine who talked about this amazing adult program at All About Dance. Two days later I walked into Jessica's (the owner's) studio. She had only been open for a year. And everything was bright and pink and orange and 100% my vibe. I walked up to the desk and gave her my resume, and said I really want to grow your childrens program.

We chatted and hit it off, and I did a sample class the next day and then started working for her. I taught for her for a full year and at the end of that year we were just loving our connection with one another, and that's when we started talking about a partnership and what that would look like.

We became partners, and I feel like the rest is history. The studio has grown a ton, and in 2010 we moved to a new location. Now we have seven studios within that location and it's just been an amazing journey to have something that you really wanted in life, come to fruition.

Also being in a partnership where I just think we match each other as far as our strengths and weaknesses, now the sky's the limit. We're both on the same track about where we want to go with the business and now we're at the point where we're not teaching as much, so we're really focusing on that. We are looking at different revenue streams, other locations, and just bringing dance to the world.

WHAT IS YOUR BIG 'WHY'?

When working with children, there's so much competition out there for them at such a young age so it's really important to me that we are continually instilling the love of the people around them, and showing that we really do care about them as a whole. We want to nurture them as people, and it just happens to be through dance that they are able to express themselves.

I truly believe that for many of the children we work with, that can make all the difference not only now, but throughout their lives as they grow. It always comes back to that, and it's something that the parents always compliment us on – how much we really give to them in class. So much more than just the dance technique.

Once they go into our company program, they spend so many hours at the studio that the expectation from the parents is that we are still giving them more than just movement and dance and technique.

I really want to be a part of the puzzle piece that gives them something to make them stand out as a person, through dance.

WHAT ARE SOME OF THE PRACTICAL THINGS YOU DO INSIDE THE CLASSROOM TO NURTURE THIS HOLISTIC APPROACH TO THE DANCERS?

One of the big things we expose our students to from a very young age is journaling, even if they are still just learning to read and write. We take it back to the very basics by asking them questions like, 'What words come to mind when you're in the studio?' or 'What does it feel like when you're dancing?' We also ask them what goals they have both in dancing and also the bigger picture stuff that includes their goals as a person.

Our teachers do a lot of interactive things in the beginning of class as well. It's all about connecting with dancers when they come in, and to build those relationships with their peers. We actively teach them about teamwork and support, and sometimes we'll do a beginning of class, or end of class meditation that is centered around whatever the theme for that day is. It's a really helpful tool in getting our students to start their class focusing on that, and then end with that same intention.

We always have a criteria that they work on that isn't always technique-based. Sometimes it is, but sometimes it's as simple as, 'Did you come to class today prepared?' Or it may be, 'Who's the kindest friend today?' Dance is a safe place for them and we try to just really remind them that they can leave everything outside the studio when they come in here each day and it's a fresh start.

Recently we have started inviting our seniors who graduate to bring them back to the studio and to share their life experiences once they go to college.

WHO INSPIRES YOU IN BUSINESS?

Being part of the Dance Studio Owners Inner Circle and you and the rest of the team has been huge for me.

There's definitely my husband, too. He runs a successful business himself, and he just is so great about giving me a totally different perspective when I'm feeling buried. He has a property management company, so he deals with people all throughout Chicago, and he just lets any craziness or stress roll off his shoulders. He's so resilient and I'm trying to work with him on teaching that to our children because that's such a great quality to have. It's a lost quality, especially in my generation, and with owning a business you have to be able to pick yourself back up and just keep going. He's always there for me, and always just giving me really great advice in how to do better and be stronger.

WHAT HAS CHANGED THE MOST FOR YOU IN YOUR BUSINESS JOURNEY OVER THE LAST TEN YEARS?

I definitely think the fun aspect of dance which was something that was really important to Jessica when I came in. For a long time the general focus on dance studios was around technique, competition and serious training. Or on the flip-side, there were studios who were purely recreational. During our first five years, from 2005 to 2010, we saw a lot of studios hop on the 'fun' bandwagon through their marketing and websites. 'We make dance fun'.

That's when the challenge came, on how do we shift from giving them love, nurture, fun in the beginning, but also that we make disciplined dance instruction fun through love, creativity, and community.

We really wanted to be that studio because it's important if we're going to bring in as many children as we can, to offer a variety of dance. Because every child is different and they are going to have different strengths. And even though, yes, ballet is a core technique for a

technical dancer, now we're finding that we're shifting our programs to meet the needs of our clients because we might have a student that is amazing at hip hop.

For us, we're just really trying to hit home that at the basic level for recreational, fun, well rounded, and then the building blocks of what that looks like once they get into our highest competitive level. In every aspect of our business, we are finding out what that means in a recreational program, in a pre-company and in competitive stance, and how that aligns with our values.

WHAT MAKES ALL ABOUT DANCE SO UNIQUE?

Staying on the forefront of not only the dance education part of it, and the technique and the up and coming teachers and choreographers in the community, but also what's happening at the schools. And what's happening developmentally at each age group, and trying to combine those at our studio. We can't turn our backs to issues that are happening out in the communities or at schools because the children are bringing those in to the dance studio.

We have nine core values, and are always working with our teachers to make sure that there's something about each of our core values or at least one. We pick one to focus on each month that they are giving to the students, so that it seems like a synergistic idea in the studio. Whether you're two or if you're 18, you are a part of the value that we are promoting that month as a community.

WHAT ARE SOME OF THE BIGGEST BUSINESS DECISIONS YOU'VE MADE THAT HAVE IMPACTED ON THE GROWTH OF YOUR STUDIO?

Knowing our marketplace and not jumping on moving to a new location or adding studios too soon are some examples of how we've really been patient in watching our growth. When moving from our previous studio location to our current one, we grew really quickly just by the matter of having more space and more availability to give to clients. Within that location, we've taken our time to fit-out the building and not just jump in there with seven studios if we didn't have the class capacity to profit.

Also re-looking at the organization and business structure of everything. Jessica and I were so involved in the classroom for nine years, that it was critical for us to start taking a step back and looking at the customer experience and seeing what that looks like for them. We really started listening to the clients and giving them what they wanted, and that led us to work with an internal consultant at the time and assess our core values and mission statement, and really bring our partnership together with what we wanted for the business.

Lastly, being a part of this Dance Studio Owners Inner Circle has been huge because when you do grow so rapidly, you let go of all the little things that are not in place. Whether the goal is about growth, or scaling, or expanding to more locations, we can't just sit with everything in our brain. That's the point that we're filtering through now, which is so important because we do have big dreams and it's just a matter of us sticking to those goals and actually seeing them come to fruition.

WHAT IS YOUR FAVORITE PIECE OF BUSINESS ADVICE?

Definitely don't sweat the small stuff. I know that's a very cliché saying, but for me personally when I first became a business owner, I definitely took everything personally. And especially in working with parents and clients, and being young when I first started.

You think the parents have all of the knowledge and the power. And quickly taking a stance in that and believing in myself and believing in all the other people around us has made a tremendous difference.

As a business owner, just really taking a step back and still believing in myself and knowing that what I'm giving our teachers in the best education. What we're learning in the Dance Studio Owners Inner Circle is so valuable because a teacher who may not have been in the corporate world is not going to gain those leadership skills anywhere else. A lot of times, they are only focusing on what's going on in the classroom. And to make them a really great person, teacher, leader, all of those things, it starts with us, the studio owners.

WHAT ARE YOUR BIGGEST STRENGTHS AS A CEO?

My strengths as a CEO are definitely consistency and just a calm nature about myself. I really try to listen to our employees and what their needs are. And also, give them autonomy to grow and to succeed and to have the opportunity to do what they do best. I think also being empathetic. When we work with women, which most of our studio is, you have to take feelings into consideration.

It's been good for me being able to work remotely from my studio, because it's given me the opportunity to learn to delegate and step back and say, okay, if I do want this person to be great in their role, then I need to give them the opportunity to actually do these tasks, and take the time to train them.

We use tools like Asana and Slack that now a lot of businesses are using are extremely helpful because it really does keep communication and expectations between us streamlined and consistent. Some people don't even realize that I'm not actually living in Chicago where the studio is, which is great because it shows that those systems are really working.

For me and my personality, being able to be removed from the studio and having that time has been really great in seeing what my team actually needs to thrive and to do their job, and for me not to micromanage.

HOW HAS YOUR EXPERIENCE IN THE CORPORATE WORLD IMPACTED ON YOUR ROLE AS A DANCE STUDIO OWNER?

I do value coming from the corporate world and having that background of being under the umbrella of an owner that was super hands-on and working with all different departments within that business, and knowing what that structure feels like. Sitting in a meeting and being the lowest one on the totem pole and having to be professional and learn to listen, to learn where my place was in that company, was very valuable.

It also showed me how I could grow, and what I had to do to get to the next level. It taught me really great things about client relations because it was advertising and trying to sell our product, and listen a lot to the client, what their needs were while providing them with a great product.

It's given Jessica and I a launch pad for teaching our directors and teachers, giving them more skills besides just teaching dance, so that if they decide that they want to open up a franchise of All About Dance or do something on their own, that we're providing them with those skills too. So many teachers come right out of college and they have never sat in a boardroom, or in a meeting, or had to deal with a bunch of other employees on an analytical level.

They walk into a studio, and they get to do what they want to do.

Learning to share spaces, be respectful, be professional and reflect on what that looks like within our community is huge.

WHAT ARE YOUR FAVORITE RETENTION STRATEGIES ONCE A STUDENT HAS ENROLLED AT ALL ABOUT DANCE?

Our biggest thing is just the structure of the flow of our programming. We start with our Mommy and Me programming where we are bringing in the caregiver or the parent with them. We are really starting from that point of inception when they first come into the studio and see that this is what we're about. It is not just your typical song and dance program.

We're teaching these skills to the children, and we also want you to be part of our community and here's how. Instilling that, because they are in the classroom, we're getting to talk to them face to face.

Then those children that start in that program before going into our three plus recreational program do so much better. They are so much more confident going into the classroom, they already know our community and have a certain comfort level. We do progress reports twice a year just to give the parents an idea of how their child is doing, and recommending where we think they should go from there.

We ask our teachers to do a little personal blurb on every child. It can be something simple when they are really little, but this was the first year we got a lot of compliments on that. We bring the parents in twice a year too, into the classroom to do a showcase for them as well as our recital.

We have a Starlet program, our pre-company programs that they can audition for once they are six, and these dancers have a whole uniform. We have the Starlet Board, they get their own tank top and All About Dance gear to go along with it. And that has been huge for us to have something to aspire for, and something to show real progression.

The camaraderie around that is huge. We take everybody into that program as long as they are dedicated and focused. It's not a skilled, technical audition yet.

The final thing is that once they are 12 at our studio, they can apply to go to our Haiti dance camp. We do that every summer in July, we've been doing it for the past four years with Fondation Enfant Jesus (FEJ). It is the organization that my husband and I adopted our son through, so holds a very special place in our hearts as well as the hearts of our dance community.

Successful applicants from our studio come down for a week to a school in Haiti where we do a dance camp, and we've had 50 to 100 children each year and they get chosen to come to the camp based on how well they do in school.

We have six to 14 year-old children from Haiti attending, and we do meals for them twice a day, arts and crafts and then we do a whole dance camp, where they will perform at the end of the week. Our students that come down with us assist us as teachers, and get to work with the children. It's been a really great experience. They come back and then each year, the children who've gone before talk about it at the recital, and we raise funds for the project every year.

WHAT HAS BEEN YOUR BIGGEST LESSON SINCE JOINING THIS AMAZING BUSINESS PARTNERSHIP?

Making sure that studio owners, or anybody in the dance industry, find like-minded mentors and people that they can talk with. Owning a dance studio is hard. And it's unlike any other corporation out there, so you start to feel 'less than' when you're speaking to other business owners sometimes. I don't think they maybe take our business as seriously, and so it's nice to have other people in the industry that you can talk to that totally get it.

It's important to have people who are on that same wavelength and can continue pushing you along and supporting you. And the ideas out there to share – we're all so creative, it's amazing to be able to pull from that and have that energy around this industry. I really do think the industry's making a shift, and I love that we've been kind of on the forefront of that in bringing the fun back to dance, no matter what level you are at.

I would just say to continue down that path, and to believe in the fact that our product is more than just steps. It's more than just movement. And unlike any other activity, dance is such a form of expression. It's a way that these children individually or in a group are going to be able to express themselves through dance.

DANCE STUDIO SECRETS BONUS –
LEARN HOW SHANNON IMPROVED HER LEADERSHIP SKILLS
WHILE ALSO GAINING CLARITY ON HER STUDIO GROWTH
PLAN IN OUR EXCLUSIVE BONUS INTERVIEW
DSOA.COM/SHANNON

Chapter Twenty-Two
DON'T WAIT TO ELEVATE

Congratulations for making it to the very end of *Dance Studio Secrets*. In the fast-paced, high distraction, low attention span world that we live in today, getting to the end of this book shows me that you have what it takes to build a successful dance studio. You're committed to your vision of success and you're not afraid to do the work.

As you would have noticed throughout the book, building a successful studio isn't easy and doesn't just happen by accident. One big pattern you would have seen throughout the journeys shared by our studio owners is that they all had guidance from mentors along the way. No one has gone it alone.

Well, many have gone it alone – but they are not in this book. Unfortunately, in our industry, many studio owners end up closing their business due to burnout.

I hope after reading these inspiring stories that you feel ready to take that leap and step into the role of the CEO of your studio.

But to make that happen, you need more than motivation and an inspiring story. That will only get you so far and what I want for you is a plan that will last you for years to come.

First, take all of your ideas from this book and categorize them in to three areas:

1.   To Do – Only ideas that support your current 90 day goals (more on this below)

2.   Great Ideas – All the other great ideas you heard that don't relate to your current 90 day goals

3.   Resources & Tools – List books, mentors, software, etc. you noted down

Then you need to start at the beginning of the planning process. First up – you need to build a three year vision for your studio, followed by a 12 month and 90 day plan.

This is phase one of achieving success in your studio, the very important planning stage! If you would like help from my team and I on achieving your goals, then I would love to see you join us as a member of the Dance Studio Owners Association.

Go to www.dsoa.com/programs for the details on our Association and Inner Circle membership options.

DANCE STUDIO SECRETS BONUS –
DOWNLOAD OUR COMPLETE '65 WAYS TO BUILD A THRIVING STUDIO' CHECKLIST AT
DSOA.COM/65WAYS

ACKNOWLEDGEMENTS

Before I leave you, I want to thank a few people that have made this book happen.

Mel Rufus – five years ago you applied to do a writing job for our company when it was just me and one other team member. I'm so grateful to have you part of team DSOA. Your commitment to our members and our mission is inspiring. Without you, this book would not exist. Thank you so much for working with our members to share their stories which will inspire thousands of studio owners around the globe. You are one in a million and I'm honored to not only call you a work buddy but an amazing friend.

DSOA Team – thank you to Jessica, Arun, Reagan, Sheree and Jason for continuing to lift the barre on the work that we do at DSOA. Your care, creativity and cutting-edge thinking ensures we deliver the best training and experience for our members. I appreciate each of you and couldn't imagine DOSA without you!

My Wisdom Circle – I wouldn't be where I am today without the continual support from my amazing family and friends who encourage me daily to achieve my goals. Mum, Alejandro, Michael, Tracy, Padma, Christina and Robert. Thank you for your daily belief in me.

Our Members – the heroes in this story. Our Inner Circle members are some of the most incredible human beings I've ever met. They show up each day and give 100% to their team, customers and their families at home. Your commitment to growth is beyond inspiring and I'm so honored and grateful daily that you have selected us here at DSOA to walk your studio success path with you.

And lastly I want to thank you, the reader. I'm wishing you every success in your journey to becoming the go-to studio in your area!

Much love,

Clint

ABOUT THE AUTHOR – CLINT SALTER

By age 28, Clint had created, built and sold three businesses, two of them in dance. He started dancing jazz at age nine before moving on to tap, ballet and hip hop. Then, in a fortuitous turn of events, a former teacher of his sold her studio. Clint actually had parents approaching him to ask if he would teach their children — and open up his own Dance Studio. So, at the ripe age of 16, Clint and a friend started their own studio.

It started as a small studio, with just 30 students. Fast-forward five years and it was operating six days a week, with a total enrollment of a few hundred students and classes running at capacity. Clint and his partner had built a booming business — and Clint was only 21. Around that time, Clint decided to sell his half of the studio to his partner as he prepared to start working at the top celebrity agency in Australia, managing some of the biggest names in television and media.

Over the five years Clint was with the talent agency, he was responsible for pitching ideas and securing commercial endorsements, licensing, publishing, television, radio and speaking deals for his stable of high-profile clients. During this time, Clint also created DanceLife, Australia's largest community for dancers and performers. In four years of operation, DanceLife became Australia's bible of all things dance: an online resource for dancers, a large dance competition and a learn-to-dance program for primary and high schools. Clint sold DanceLife after four years to take an opportunity to be the Touring Manager for the musical *Jersey Boys*, where he travelled internationally while managing a team of 56 people.

After spending so much time working at the agency and running his businesses, Clint decided he wanted to share with dance studio owners the knowledge he'd accumulated. He wanted to help studio owners learn how to design their lives and create a thriving, profitable studio that allowed them to spend more time working 'on' rather than 'in' the business, something that is accomplished by creating a rock-solid automated business model as well as running a year-long student attraction and retention strategy. Clint is the Founder of the Dance Studio Owners Association and Studio Success Formula, the #1 Business Growth Program for dance studio owners where he offers mentoring and online training programs to help studio owners turn their passion for dance into a profitable business that makes a big difference in the lives of their dance families.

For more information about the Dance Studio Owners Association go to:

WWW.DOSA.COM

Printed in Great Britain
by Amazon

37494751R00108